# SUN YAT SEN

## SUN YAT SEN

Inscriptions on the original, written by Sun Yat Sen, read:
right, "Brother Ai for preservation"; left, "Respectfully
given by Sun Wen."

# SUN YAT SEN

## LIBERATOR OF CHINA

BY

HENRY BOND RESTARICK

WITH A PREFACE BY
KENNETH SCOTT LATOURETTE

NEW HAVEN
YALE UNIVERSITY PRESS
LONDON · HUMPHREY MILFORD · OXFORD UNIVERSITY PRESS
1931

Copyright, 1931, by Yale University Press
Printed in the United States of America

All rights reserved. This book may not be reproduced, in whole or in part, in any form, except by written permission from the publishers.

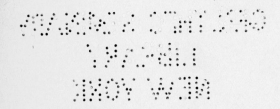

TO MY CHINESE FRIENDS
IN HAWAII AND CHINA

"But if any man undertakes to write a history that has to be collected from observation and the reading of works not easy to be got at in all places, for him undoubtedly it is in the first place and above all things most necessary to reside in some city of good note, where he may have plenty of all sorts of books, and, on enquiry, may hear and inform himself of such particulars, as, having escaped the pens of writers, are most faithfully preserved in the memories of men, lest his work be deficient in many things, even those which it can least dispense with."                                     Plutarch.

For one who writes the life of Sun Yat Sen, Honolulu fulfils these requirements. In the catalogue of the Library of Hawaii there are six hundred titles under the heading of China, and there are now living in Honolulu reliable men of excellent memory who knew Sun Yat Sen from his boyhood until his death.                                     H. B. R.

# Preface

SUN YAT SEN was one of the outstanding figures of his generation. No other single individual of his time has so profoundly influenced the Chinese. Probably only three or four of his contemporaries have had so great an effect upon the political and social thinking of as many people. Judged by this standard, he ranks with Wilson, Lenin, and Gandhi. Wilson molded the ideals which helped to win the World War and more than any other man was responsible for the League of Nations; Lenin embodied the purposes and program of the Russian Revolution; Gandhi has led and profoundly modified Indian nationalism; Sun Yat Sen was the outstanding figure in the political revolution through which China has been passing, and his teachings are still revered—at least outwardly—by the party which continues to be dominant in the largest fairly homogeneous group of mankind.

It is too early to write a definitive biography of Dr. Sun. The necessary materials have not been gathered, emotional reactions toward Dr. Sun are too strong to permit of reasonable objectivity, and not enough time has elapsed since his death fully to appraise his place in the history of his nation. He is, moreover, a strangely enigmatic and contradictory figure. His countrymen themselves are divided over the relative importance of Chinese and foreign influences on his teachings. Some of his analyses of the causes of Chinese distress seem very remote from the facts, and many of his suggestions for the reorganization of the nation are almost naïvely impracticable; yet more than any other single individual he brought idealism into the sordid struggle of the militarists in the civil wars which have wracked the nation most of the time since 1917. His teachings still serve to lift Chinese politics above the level of crass selfishness—to the slight degree to which that has been done. As an administrator he very largely failed in maintaining ordered government and had difficulty even in retaining a foothold in Canton, where he spent more time than in any other city of China; yet he was the organizer of the movement which overthrew the Manchus and set up the Republic, and the party of which he was the head is the governing body of China and is the most powerful organization which China has known for the past fifteen years. No more fascinating subject could be found for a great biography.

Bishop Restarick has not attempted to write this biography. He has modestly contented himself mainly with gathering material concerning Dr. Sun's earlier years. He has, to be sure, included a brief summary of the already well-known facts about Dr. Sun's career after the Revolution of 1911. This, however, is chiefly for readers to whom these may not already be familiar. As will be readily seen, the great value of the book lies in the diligence with which information has been collected from those who knew Dr. Sun intimately before the time when, in 1911, he suddenly rose to worldwide recognition. Most of this, as Bishop Restarick says, has never before appeared in print. More than any other we now have, the book throws light on the influences which shaped Dr. Sun in his youth and early manhood. Not only will it prove fascinating to the general reader and to all those interested in Dr. Sun, but it is safe to say that it will make an important contribution to any really satisfying future biography of its subject.

KENNETH SCOTT LATOURETTE.

*Yale University,*
*June, 1931.*

# Author's Preface

THIS book has been written with the desire of presenting a truthful account of Sun Yat Sen, from his birth and boyhood to the end of his strange turbulent career. All recent books on China mention him; but statements about his early years, as a rule, are singularly inaccurate and misleading. Books which deal more fully with his life also contain strange errors which show lack of information, and sometimes it is evident that the writers were misled, probably for a purpose. The purpose of this account is to throw new light on his career, and particularly upon its earlier phases; the information in the later sections which serve to round out the story is comparatively familiar.

For twenty-eight years I have known intimately several Chinese who were closely associated with Sun Yat Sen from his boyhood until his death. These have been annoyed by the erroneous stories appearing in books about their friend and hero. Some of them came to me and said that, Dr. Sun having died, they were willing to give me information which they had on several occasions refused to persons who had interviewed them. They believed that the time had come when the truth should be known, and they asked me to write the life of Sun Yat Sen.

The task has not been an easy one, and it has been

especially difficult to obtain correct dates. There are no written records of his youth, and no letters of his have been preserved dealing with his school days or with many of his activities, including some of his numerous escapes from capture. Information given orally has been checked by the testimony of several persons, and every effort has been made to secure accuracy.

Much of what I have written has never appeared in print. Some things my Chinese friends did not like to have printed; but I told them that this was a biography of Sun Yat Sen, not designed to deck him with a halo of legendary glamor but to present the man as he was, a human being with faults as well as virtues.

Before undertaking the work I wrote to Sun Fo, the son of Sun Yat Sen, asking him for information concerning his father. His reply was as follows:

Chief Commissioner's Office,
Canton, July 26, 1926.

Bishop Henry B. Restarick,
    1715 Anapuni Street,
    Honolulu, Hawaii.

Dear Sir:
    Your letter of the 14th April interested me very much. I am pleased to learn that you are so much interested in the life of my father, Sun Yat Sen, as to make special efforts to secure true facts in regard thereto.
    It is generally felt by authors, foreign as well as Chinese, that there is great difficulty in getting reliable sources of information to write an accurate biography of my father, as the existing books are most unsatisfactory. You are, however,

fortunate in having secured persons right in Honolulu who can give you true accounts of his boyhood and career.

I regret there is not much material available that I can suggest for your reference, but I shall be glad to answer as fully as I can the questions you send me, and would like to read over your manuscript when it is finished.

Yours truly,

[*Signed*] SUN FO.

In my letter to Sun Fo I had mentioned the names of the Chinese who were ready to give me information concerning his father, and his reply shows that from long acquaintance with them he knew they were truthful and reliable men.

This book is written neither to advocate nor to oppose the doctrines of Sun Yat Sen. It is not a history of China or an account of the customs of the people, and reference to these will be made only when it is deemed necessary to the right understanding of an occurrence. It is a plain story of Sun Yat Sen, the Revolutionist, or as he is now often called, the Father of the Republic of China.

I wish to express my indebtedness to the following persons who have given me valuable assistance.

Luke Chan was born in the same village as Sun Yat Sen, and was an intimate friend of the Sun family. He was Dr. Sun's agent in Honolulu, and in 1911 was living in the same house with him at Nanking when he resigned from the presidency. Mr. Chan is a Chinese scholar and a follower of Confucius. He has been the trusted employee of a large American business firm in Honolulu for many years.

Chang Chau was the sworn brother of Sun Yat Sen, and was with him in two of his escapes from capture. He is a public notary of the Territory of Hawaii, and is a well-known man of affairs.

Chang Kun Ai, generally known as C. K. Ai (pronounced Ah-ee), was the schoolmate of Sun Yat Sen and his lifelong friend and supporter. He is a prosperous business man in Honolulu, and is respected by the whole community.

Ho Fon presided at the first meeting of the revolutionists held in Honolulu, and was closely associated with Sun Yat Sen until his death. He was employed by an American bank in Honolulu for thirty years.

Tong Phong was baptized at the same time as Sun Yat Sen in Hongkong, and was his intimate friend. He is now President of the Chinese-American Bank in Honolulu.

Dr. Mon Fa Chung is a graduate of Harvard College and Harvard Medical School, and was in Peking when Sun Yat Sen died. He was present at the exploratory operation which Dr. Sun underwent at the Peking Medical Hospital, just before he died.

Dr. H. N. Kinnear and his wife were residents of southern China for forty years. Dr. Sun was once a patient of Dr. Kinnear.

I am also indebted to Shao Chang Lee, professor of

Chinese language and literature at the University of Hawaii, for his kind assistance in the translation of Chinese documents and for information as to the meaning of Chinese names.

Five of those named have read the entire manuscript and others have read portions of it, and their corrections and suggestions have been of great value.

---

In writing Chinese names, the family name, which comes first, is of course always retained, while the two given names which follow may be changed many times. Chinese scholars, to whom I have referred the matter, prefer to begin each name with a capital, using no hyphen, on the ground that each name is represented by a different character and one is not necessarily connected with the other. Although at present common usage employs the hyphen between given names, the Chinese preference has been observed in the form of all names in this book, and the name perhaps more familiar as Sun Yat-sen appears as Sun Yat Sen.

H. B. R.

*Honolulu, Hawaii,*
*June, 1931.*

# Contents

PREFACE BY KENNETH SCOTT LATOURETTE     ix

AUTHOR'S PREFACE     xiii

ILLUSTRATIONS     xxi

I. THE BIRTHPLACE OF SUN YAT SEN     1

II. IN HAWAII     11

III. TAI CHEONG RETURNS TO CHINA     21

IV. TAI CHEONG BECOMES SUN YAT SEN     27

V. THE FIRST ATTEMPT AT REVOLUTION     39

VI. IN HONOLULU, THE UNITED STATES, AND
ENGLAND     47

VII. TRAVELS     55

VIII. THE ATTEMPTED REVOLT OF 1900     65

IX. ABROAD AGAIN     73

X. THE UNLUCKY PLAN OF REVOLT IN 1904     81

XI. NEW PREPARATIONS FOR REVOLUTION     89

XII. THE FIRST TRIUMPH     97

XIII. TREACHERY AND DISILLUSIONMENT     109

XIV. SUN YAT SEN AND HIS FAMILY     125

XV. A FRESH BEGINNING IN CANTON     133

XVI. THE LAST YEARS     149

BIBLIOGRAPHY     161

INDEX     163

# Illustrations

SUN YAT SEN                                    frontispiece

CHANG CHAU                          facing page    4

LUKE CHAN                                           4

CHOY HUNG. THE VILLAGE WHERE SUN YAT SEN
    WAS BORN                                       24

THE SIX NAMES OF SUN YAT SEN                       36

SUN YAT SEN AT THE MING TOMBS                     114

SUN YAT SEN AND SUNG HING LING                    130

SUN YAT SEN AS GENERALISSIMO                      134

CHINESE REVOLUTIONISTS IN JAPAN                   138

SUN YAT SEN, 1925                                 152

# SUN YAT SEN

## CHAPTER I

## The Birthplace of Sun Yat Sen

### His Boyhood and His Boy Name, Tai Cheong

THE early life of men who become prominent in the world's affairs, their place of birth, parentage, environment, and education, are always important influences in their development.

Sun Yat Sen, who may certainly be called the Revolutionist, was born in the village of Choy Hung, in the province of Kwangtung, China. It is situated about forty miles from Canton, a short distance from the estuary of the Canton or Pearl River. The year of his birth is variously given by writers, but it took place in 1866 and the day was November 2. The difference in dates given for his birth no doubt arises from the fact that he generally gave his age according to Chinese reckoning, which is not the same as ours. At whatever time of the year a child is born, on the first day of the Chinese New Year he is said to be one year old. This is the case even if he is born the day before the festival; and since the date of the Chinese New Year's Day depends upon the moon, there may be a difference of a year between their reckoning of age and ours.

Since different dates are given in publications, it may be well to know what Sun Yat Sen himself said. On the last anniversary of his birth which he spent in Canton, shortly before his death, he entertained a few friends at dinner. Among them was Eugene Chen, who was his personal secretary during the last three years of his life. Mr. Chen wrote:[1]

At this dinner, in answer to a question, Dr. Sun made the statement that he was on that day fifty-eight years old, calculating in the foreign style, having been born in Choy Hung, province of Kwangtung, on November 2, 1866, which corresponds to the 25th day of the 9th moon, in the fifth year of the Emperor Tung Tai.

His father's name was Sun Tat Sung, Sun being the family name which Chinese custom places first. He was a rice farmer, who did not own the land which he cultivated, but rented it, paying yearly about one-half of the crop. His house, like most of those in the village, was built of mud and lime mixed with rice straw, which made a substantial dwelling. The roof and the floors were of tiles. Light and air were admitted through openings which were closed with wooden shutters when the weather was cold or windy. The furniture was simple, consisting of a table, chairs, and bedsteads; the Chinese do not sit or sleep on the floor as the Japanese do. Such is the description of the house given by those who knew it well.

In this house was born the boy who was to have his name known all over the world, as the chief instrument in arousing the Chinese from the lethargy of the ages.

His mother was a little-footed woman, for she was a Punti, and as such she looked down upon the Hakka women who did not, as a rule, bind their feet. Hakka means a stranger; many years ago, these people came from the north and occupied lands in Kwangtung. They spoke a different dialect.

[1] A communication to a Shanghai paper, the *China Press*, signed by Eugene Chen.

When she gave birth to a son on November 2, 1866, a baby name was soon given him, according to custom. This name usually expresses some wish for the future of the child, or is taken from some incident connected with his birth or with the time immediately preceding it. Several names were suggested, but the mother insisted that he be called Tai Cheong, and by this name the future Sun Yat Sen was known during his entire boyhood, both at home and at school.

The reason that she chose this name she told in 1896, in Honolulu, where she went after the failure of Sun's first attempt at insurrection in 1895. With Dr. Sun's wife and her three children, she had fled to Hongkong, fearful lest the authorities should wreak vengeance on the rebel's family. She was then a widow and wanted to go to Hawaii, where her oldest son, Ah Mi, was prospering. At this time Luke Chan, an old friend of the family, had gone to China to procure a wife; and as he was returning to Honolulu, the Sun family was placed in his care.

On landing, the women and children went to the house of friends of Dr. Sun, named Chang; there they were cared for until they could go to the island of Maui where Ah Mi then lived. The widow was in great distress because of her exile from her old home, and often in her Punti dialect would give vent to her feelings and say: "Oh, Tai Cheong! Why did you bring this trouble on your family? Why did you not live peaceably in Choy Hung instead of making all this disturbance?"

Hearing this often repeated, Chang Chau, one of the household, asked her why she kept calling her son Tai Cheong, a name he had not heard applied to him before. Her answer was this story:

About a month before Yat Sen was born I had a dream which greatly troubled me. There came to me the great god Buck Dai. He had his hair hanging down as our people wear it in time of sorrow. He was weeping and looked at me as if he were very much worried. When I awoke the thought came to me that the god was afraid the child which I was soon to bring into the world would cause him some injury. When the child was born I chose the name Tai Cheong, and I have always called him that, and if he had lived up to its meaning he would never have brought this trouble upon his family. Oh Tai Cheong! Why did you take up with the ways of the foreign people?

The reason of the widow's lament requires explanation. To know the meaning of the words forming the boy's name, a Chinese would have to see the characters which represent the idea. Reading them on the family scroll in Choy Hung, a Chinese scholar would at once perceive their significance. Tai (or Dai) is god, and Cheong, used in this connection, conveys the idea of one who serves.

The god who appeared to the mother in her dream was the central one of the three in the village temple, whose name was Buck Dai. He had long hair, which in the dream was hanging about his face. In giving her son the name she was dedicating him to the service of this god. When he grew up, as will be told, he repudiated it by a remarkable act.

The boyhood of Tai Cheong was like that of millions of boys in China. Choy Hung was a typical Chinese village containing about five hundred inhabitants. Its people were singularly progressive, for all the boys attended the school supported by the villagers. In a country where nine persons out of ten are illiterate, this is remarkable. But stranger still was the fact that, con-

## LUKE CHAN

Born in the same village as Sun Yat Sen and an intimate friend of the family, who was with Dr. Sun at Nanking when he was President of the Republic of China.

## CHANG CHAU

The sworn brother of Sun Yat Sen who was with him in two rebellions and his companion in two of his escapes.

trary to the general custom, girls attended the school as well as boys, if their parents desired it.

When Tai Cheong went to this school, the teacher was an accomplished Chinese scholar. Instruction was, of course, carried on in the old way, the pupils studying out loud and reciting one by one with backs turned to the teacher. They learned the names of the characters, but did not know their meaning until later. They learned nothing of the outside world nor anything of modern knowledge. School began at about six o'clock in the morning, in summer, and continued until five o'clock in the afternoon, and there were few holidays, except some days at the beginning of the New Year.

When Tai Cheong left this school, he was about thirteen years old and he knew about three thousand characters. He never attended any other Chinese school, and was not an advanced Chinese scholar, though he was very studious and acquired a knowledge of many more characters as he grew older.

At that time there was no Christian mission at Choy Hung, so that the boy had no opportunity to learn any English there. The people were without exception Confucians; they worshiped in the temple and honored the shades of their ancestors on memorial days. These facts need to be stated because it has been widely reported in publications that the boy's father was an agent for the London Missionary Society and that Tai Cheong learned English in his native village. Sun Tat Sung was an earnest Confucian and was greatly disturbed when his son expressed his desire to be baptized, a few years after he left China.

Inquiry is often made as to where Sun Yat Sen got his revolutionary ideas. It certainly was not in his native village. But some things the boy must have heard. The Cantonese hated the Manchu rulers, holding them to be usurpers and not of the Chinese race. The village folk were afraid to talk on such matters openly, and the older men warned the younger ones of the danger of expressing their opinions, for there were spies abroad. But he must have heard of the Taiping Rebellion which had come to an end only a short time before he was born; in it many Cantonese were implicated.

It was when Tai Cheong was about thirteen years old that his older brother, Ah Mi, who was doing well in the Hawaiian Islands, wrote to his father urging him to send the younger son to Honolulu. Ah Mi was an enterprising man and saw the advantage of a modern education, which he promised his young brother should have if he could come. As many Chinese were going to Hawaii at that time, there was no difficulty in sending him. Glowing accounts had been heard from those who had gone to the Hawaiian Islands; and, like others, Sun Tat Sung looked upon Hawaii as the land of opportunity. It was arranged that Tai Cheong should be sent to join his brother.

The story would not be complete without notice of the story, often repeated in books and papers, that Sun Yat Sen was born in Hawaii and was therefore a citizen of the United States.

At the time when the United States annexed the Republic of Hawaii by treaty, an organic act was passed by Congress, in 1898; and under its provisions all who had been born in Hawaii prior to that date were recognized as citizens of the United States of America.

In view of the facts already given, how did the story

originate that Sun Yat Sen was born in Hawaii? The answer is plain. In 1904, Sun Yat Sen obtained a certificate that he was born in the Hawaiian Islands. The older Chinese in Honolulu knew at the time that it was secured by fraud; but out of sympathy for Dr. Sun and knowing that in traveling about he was in danger of his life, they kept quiet. A copy of the birth certificate is here given.

## DEPOSITION OF HAWAIIAN BIRTH
### SUN YAT SEN.

Adult No. 25. ⎫
Territory of Hawaii ⎬
Island of Oahu. ⎭

I, Sun Yat Sen, being first duly sworn, depose and say that to the best of my knowledge and belief, I was born at Waimanu, Ewa, Oahu, on the 24th day of November, 1870; that I am a physician, practicing at present at Kula, Island of Maui; that I make my home at said Kula; that my father, Sun Tat Sung, went to China in 1874, and died there about eight years later; and that this affidavit is made for the purpose of identifying myself; and as a further proof of my Hawaiian birth, that the photograph attached is a good likeness of me at this time.

[Signed] SUN YAT SEN.

Subscribed and sworn to
before me this ninth day of March, A.D. 1904.

[Seal] [Signed] KATE KELLY.

Notary Public, First Judicial Circuit,
Territory of Hawaii.

This is to certify that I have made a thorough examination of the statements made here and am satisfied as to their accu-

racy, and that the photograph attached is a good likeness and
that the signature was made by the applicant.

[*Signed*] A. L. C. ATKINSON,
Secretary of Hawaii.

Adult No. 25.
Territory of Hawaii, } ss.
Office of the Secretary.

## TO ALL TO WHOM THESE PRESENTS SHALL COME—
### GREETING.

This is to certify that Sun Yat Sen, now residing at Kula,
Maui, T. H., whose signature is attached, has made application
No. 25, for a certificate of birth.

And that it appears from his affidavit and the evidence submitted by witnesses, that he was born in the Hawaiian Islands,
on the 24th day of November, A. D. 1870, and that the
photograph attached is a good likeness of him at this time.

In testimony whereof the Secretary of the Territory has
hereunto subscribed his name and caused the Seal of the Territory of Hawaii to be affixed.

[*Signed*] A. L. C. ATKINSON.

Done in Honolulu this 14th day of March 1904.
Signature of Sun Yat Sen,

[*Signed*] SUN YAT SEN.

Mr. Atkinson used every effort to ascertain the facts
of the birth of Sun Yat Sen, but he was deceived.
Shortly before his death in 1926 he wrote:

What you say about Dr. Sun interests me considerably.
When I was Secretary I issued to him a birth certificate. I went
to a great deal of trouble in getting evidence of his birth. The
evidence recorded in the Secretary's office when the certificate
was issued is not by any means all the evidence that I took
concerning his birth. I went thoroughly into the matter at the

time and I was satisfied from the evidence and issued the certificate.

In connection with the foregoing it should be borne in mind that at the time when the certificate was obtained, Sun Yat Sen was a refugee from China and there was a reward of half a million dollars upon his head. He was visiting his brother on the island of Maui and was preparing to go to the United States. There were spies everywhere, and several attempts were made to kidnap him. He wanted to travel unmolested in order to promote the interests of the revolution and to secure funds to carry on the propaganda for it. This he could do more freely as an American citizen than as a subject of the Chinese Empire. On Dr. Sun's part, it was a war measure. Whether his conduct was in any essential point different from that of diplomats who have often deceived to gain their ends, or any worse than the lies for propaganda told during the Great War, it is for the reader to judge.

In getting the birth certificate, I suppose he and his friends who swore falsely reasoned somewhat as Lieutenant O'Brien did, in his advice to Peter Simple, in the novel by Captain Marryat, when he said:

I know but one point on which a lie is excusable, and that is when you wish to deceive the enemy. Then your duty to your country warrants your lying till you're black in the face, and for the very reason that it goes against your grain, it becomes, as it were, a sort of virtue.

## CHAPTER II

# In Hawaii

The School Days of Tai Cheong (Later Sun Yat
Sen). He Embraces the Christian Religion

THE Sandwich Islands, as the Hawaiian group
was called for many years after their discovery
by Captain Cook in 1778, were soon known to
the Chinese. Following the discovery, trade in fur soon
began between the northwest coast of America and
Canton, in which Americans and British engaged. The
vessels employed in this trade usually called at the
Sandwich Islands for provisions and, when sandalwood
was found there, a large business developed in carrying
that wood to China. This led the Chinese to call the
Hawaiian group the Sandalwood Islands, the name
they bear in China today.

In the first half of the last century a number of
Chinese had become residents of the Hawaiian Islands,
but it was not until 1876 that they came in large numbers. Then the reciprocity treaty was signed between
the United States and Hawaii, which led to rapid development of the sugar industry. There followed a de-
mand for labor, and the Hawaiian Government sent
agents to Canton to bring over laborers under contract.
Some paid their own passage and were free to engage
in business. Among these was Ah Mi, the elder brother
of Sun Yat Sen, who soon after his arrival engaged in

rice planting on the island of Oahu, not far from Honolulu.

The elder brother is called, in Chinese, Da Ko, and he has an authority next to the father. On the arrival of his younger brother, Tai Cheong, in Honolulu, Ah Mi determined to place him in some school where he could learn English, for he knew that the important business of Hawaii was done in that language. A boarding school would be best, for there he would learn English more rapidly.

At the time there was a boarding school which was admitting a limited number of Chinese. It was conducted by the Rt. Rev. Alfred Willis of the Anglican church, and was originally intended for the better class of Hawaiian and part-Hawaiian boys. The name of the school, Iolani, had been given to it by King Kamehameha V, who was interested in the work of the church which his brother, Kamehameha IV, had been instrumental in bringing to Hawaii in 1862.

Ah Mi had an interview with the Bishop and the boy Tai Cheong entered Iolani School as a boarding scholar after the summer vacation of 1879. He knew no English at that time, so those who were his schoolmates positively assert. He was one of five Chinese boys at Iolani, all of whom wore their cues; most of them retained them while they remained in the institution.

The man who taught Tai Cheong the rudiments of English was a Hawaiian, Solomon Meheula, who had been educated in the school and was well known to the writer. All the teachers except this Hawaiian were Englishmen whom Bishop Willis had brought over to as-

sist him in the work. In this school Tai Cheong spent
about six years during the formative period of his life.

In the endeavor to show that some republican ideas
came to the boy while living in Hawaii, it has been said
that his teachers were Americans and that he was under
American influence. Nothing could be farther from the
facts. The whole atmosphere of Iolani School was intensely British. Bishop Willis and the teachers were
British by birth, education, and sympathy. English history was taught, but no American history. In fact so
English was the school that all the textbooks were
English; even the arithmetic did not deal with dollars
and cents but with pounds, shillings, and pence. The
ordinary English branches of learning were taught, and
in the higher classes a little Latin.

As a boarder, Tai Cheong was able to see few people
outside the school, so that his contact with Americans
was very slight. Hawaii was then a monarchy and the
teachers, as well as the Hawaiians who constituted the
great majority of the pupils, were loyal to the kingdom.

It is true that American influence, which had steadily
grown from the time when the American Congregational missionaries had come in 1820, was strong in the
Islands. But in the days when Tai Cheong was at Iolani
there was a strong British element, due to the fact that
there were many prominent British in business in the
Islands. There was a pro-British faction even among
the Hawaiians, who together with the British opposed
every measure which they thought would lead in time
to annexation to the United States. The English Bishop
was the spokesman for those who opposed American
aggression, and Iolani was the center of British influence.

The foregoing statement has been emphasized because it has often been asserted, or assumed, that Sun Yat Sen was indoctrinated with republican principles during his residence in Hawaii. When Dr. Sun became well known, Bishop Willis wrote on this point in his *Diocesan Magazine* in 1896:

As far as can be remembered Tai Cheong's school days gave no indication of his future career. He has left no tradition of hatching plots against magisterial authority. Nor will any one suppose that he was indoctrinated at Iolani with the love of a republican form of government, much less with the desire of revolutionizing the Celestial Kingdom after the model of the Hawaiian Republic, which was then unborn.

The last portion of the quotation will be understood when it is remembered that the Hawaiian Republic was inaugurated on July 4, 1894, and that Bishop Willis bitterly opposed it by speech and written word. He strenuously maintained that Liliuokalani was the rightful sovereign, and by this attitude incurred the dislike of Americans.

However, if this Chinese youth did not gain a knowledge of republican principles at Iolani he must have learned something of constitutional government, for Hawaii had enjoyed that advantage since 1839. He must have absorbed something of Anglo-Saxon ideals of liberty and justice, for Americans and British had been the advisers of the Hawaiian Government for many years. He must have heard from his brother and others of the way in which justice was administered by the really excellent judiciary of Hawaii. He must have seen that the workingman had a chance to improve his condition, and that he would not be robbed by officials of the proceeds of his labor. He must have had impressed upon his young mind the benefits of living in a country where life and property were safe and where men were not in constant fear of a government which was merciless toward those daring to advance ideas which they hoped would improve conditions. After living in Hawaii for some six years he must have observed the difference between Hawaii and China when he returned home in 1885. No doubt his life at Iolani greatly influenced his mind in these matters.

Those who were students at Iolani while Sun Yat Sen was there do not remember anything remarkable about him. They say he was very studious, but that is a characteristic of the Chinese who attend American or English schools. They say also that he was very good at such mathematics as were taught there. One remarked to the writer:

If Sun Yat Sen got any idea of the struggle for liberty when at Iolani, he must have obtained it from reading English history, the wresting of Magna Charta from King John or the struggle of Cromwell against the autocracy of Charles I, and the development of constitutional government in Great Britain.

All agree that he acquired a correct knowledge of English very rapidly. He heard no other language because the Hawaiian boys were not permitted to speak in their native tongue in order that they might learn English quickly. Hawaiians who had a good knowledge of English were sure of employment and many of the students became prominent in the service of the Government.

So rapid was the progress of Sun in English that on July 27, 1882, he received the second prize in English grammar.[1] It was given to him by King Kalakaua, who was present at the closing exercises of the school, as were also his sister, Princess Liliuokalani, and the Dowager Queen Emma, the widow of Kamehameha IV, all of whom took an interest in the institution. This was very good progress for a boy who, three years before, could not speak a word of English.

While none of his companions ever heard him talk about government in China, during his school life, still he did get into his heart and mind a spirit of revolt in one important particular which undoubtedly had much to do with his later revolutionary career. Through daily contact with Christian people and through the definite religious instruction which he received with all the other pupils, he became convinced of the folly of idolatry. He came to believe that much of the backwardness of China was due to superstition and the dread of evil spirits, which entered into every phase of life from birth until death, and then into the ceremonies connected with burial.

Besides the religious teaching, the boys at Iolani were obliged to attend daily morning and evening prayers in the school chapel, and on Sundays all were taken to St. Andrew's Cathedral. Bishop Willis and Mrs. Willis took a deep interest in the students, and ate in the same dining-room with them. The Bishop himself taught classes in Christian doctrine. In daily close contact with the teachers and matron, Tai Cheong could not but be impressed with the kindness and fairness of those who cared for the welfare of his body, mind, and soul.

It is no wonder therefore that he imbibed a spirit of contempt for the superstitions of idolatry and gained a

[1] The *Honolulu Advertiser,* July, 1882.

belief in one God, the Father. It is interesting to note that all of the Chinese who attended Iolani at this time became Christians, and some of them in time grew to be leaders in churches in Honolulu and elsewhere. When Tai Cheong saw his schoolmates being prepared for baptism, it was natural for him to desire to enter the Christian Church with them.

He told his brother frankly that he had become a Christian in belief and wanted to be baptized. He said he was convinced of the folly of idolatry, and ridiculed the household god that his brother, like other Chinese, had in a shrine in his house. Ah Mi was very angry; he became violent and threatened the boy. He blamed himself for sending his brother to a Christian school, and said he would take him out of Iolani and send him home.

Bishop Willis referring to this in his *Diocesan Magazine* said: "He [Tai Cheong] learned the truths of Christianity at Iolani, but was not permitted by his heathen relatives to be baptized."

Ah Mi wrote to his father telling him what had occurred, and word came back that the boy must be sent home to China at once. The letter said: "I will take this Jesus nonsense out of him when he gets home. I will see whether he will abandon the religion and customs of his ancestors and take up with the superstitions of the foreign devils." So it was that Tai Cheong left Iolani and arrangements were made for his return to China.

In 1912 an article appeared in the *Strand Magazine*, which was said to be a statement made by Sun Yat Sen in London in 1911 and has been widely quoted. It is so entirely at variance with facts given in this chapter that it is hard to imagine how it could have emanated from him, and yet it is said he authorized it. If it were not known that, when there was an important object to be gained, he made false statements, the writer would brand it as fraud perpetrated by others. The first part of the article reads:

> Up to the year 1885, when I was eighteen years of age, I led the life of any Chinese boy, except that from my father's conversion to Christianity, and his employment by the London Missionary Society, I had greater opportunity of coming in contact with English and American missionaries in Canton. An English lady became interested in me, and I learnt eventually to speak English.

The testimony of the Chinese who knew Sun Yat Sen from boyhood until his death, and the positive statements of his fellow students at Iolani, show that the foregoing story is absolutely false. C. K. Ai, who entered the school with Tai Cheong, says the boy did not know a word of English at that time. His first teacher made the same assertion.

His friends say that he could not have authorized the statements made in the *Strand Magazine* article. It will be noticed no mention is made of the years he spent in Honolulu. If Dr. Sun did authorize the article, it must have been in order to deceive the English people concerning his youth and to enlist the sympathy of English Christians. He must have wished the public of Great Britain to believe that his early life was influenced by their missionaries, and so to gain support for his revolutionary projects. Throughout his remarkable career it is evident that he did try to enlist public opinion in his favor; he was an acknowledged past-master in the art of propaganda.

It must be remembered also that Chinese generally are extremely reticent about their lives, and often mislead others in order to put an end to curiosity. A man who could swear, as a war measure, that he was born in Hawaii, would not hesitate to deceive if he thought he might gain sympathy for his cause.

## CHAPTER III

# Tai Cheong Returns to China

## He Defies the Idols, and Is Expelled from His Native Village

TAI CHEONG reached China safely, but he did not remain there long. Ah Mi had purchased a lot in Honolulu and for some reason had placed it in his brother's name. Having sold it, he sent word to Tai Cheong to return to Honolulu so that a deed might be executed.

When Tai Cheong reached Honolulu the brothers had a violent quarrel on the old subject of the younger one's abandonment of the faith of his fathers. As a result Ah Mi turned his brother out of his house. Tai Cheong sought shelter with his former schoolmate, C. K. Ai, who had just begun business in a small way. Out of sympathy for his friend, Ai took the boy in and shared with him his room, his bed, and his food.

Tai Cheong made up his mind that he would go back to China, but the question was how to obtain the money for his steerage passage. Ai gave him five dollars, another Chinese gave a like amount, and three well-to-do Americans who were interested in the Chinese contributed enough to pay his fare to Hongkong. Ai took his friend in a rowboat to a steamer outside the harbor, for at that time there was not sufficient depth of water at the entrance for a large vessel to come in.

He arrived in China about the middle of the year

1885. With his foreign learning and his new ideas of life, his friends might well wonder what would become of him. Would he be obliged to conform to the customs of his people in the matter of worship? Soon there came a crisis which answered the question, and the way he met it had much to do in determining his future.

It is fortunate that we have the story of his home-coming and the events which followed from a man who was in Choy Hung at the time. Luke Chan was a boy in the village when Tai Cheong returned. He was an intimate friend of the family and in time became an ardent supporter of Sun Yat Sen. Others corroborate his story.

There were heated discussions in the house of the Sun family, for the father was a pronounced Confucian and also—as was the common custom—practiced idolatry. Tai Cheong maintained that there was only one God, that idols were vain things, that the gods they pretended to represent could do neither harm nor good, and that until China gave up idolatrous superstition no advance could be made in the condition of the people. The father argued that China was a great nation which had existed for thousands of years, that there was no need of foreign customs or religion, that Confucius was the greatest of all teachers, and that the gods must be honored or much harm would come to the village and country.

The authority of a father was practically unlimited in China, even to the extent of putting to death a disobedient son. Tai Cheong had been brought up with that sense of filial obedience which is one of the five moral principles of Confucius governing social relationships. All who know the Chinese are aware of the honor and obedience rendered by Chinese children to parents, where the teaching of the sage has not been weakened by modern ideas learned from Americans and Europeans.

Tai Cheong must have been influenced by his residence abroad, but he could not resist the commands of his father and was obliged to conform outwardly and go to the temple and there place lighted incense sticks in the containers before the idols. He told his friends that he was like Naaman, who had to bow before the god Rimmon, though he meant nothing by it.

At this time there arrived in Choy Hung a remarkable youth named Luke Ho Tung (or Lu Ko Tung), who had a great influence over Tai Cheong, both then and later. This young man had been born in Shanghai, where his father, a native of Choy Hung, had developed a profitable business in lightering ships. On the death of his father, he had brought his body to Choy Hung so that he might be buried with his ancestors. He had returned to his mother's people in Shanghai where he pursued his studies in Chinese and English, in both of which he became so proficient that he was in time employed by the cable company as a translator. He had become a Christian and was a young man of great courage and determination, which ultimately led to his death for the cause of reform in China.

Tai Cheong and Luke Ho Tung became great friends and as they often talked on religion, Tai Cheong called the other his "doctrinal friend." Ho Tung was far better versed in Chinese history than his companion, and talked much about the corruption of the Manchu dynasty and the oppression of the people by the viceroys. Both had been under foreign influence in places where western ideas of liberty and justice prevailed. Both believed that without modern education China could never take its proper place in the world. These conversations left an indelible impression on the mind of Tai Cheong and aroused in him an implacable hatred for the Manchus.

On one occasion, when the military inspector of the district came to the village to take the quota liable for military service, Ho Tung went to see the men drill. He had seen soldiers in Shanghai and Hongkong, and to his friend he ridiculed the whole performance of the Chinese. He said that fifty men, well disciplined and armed, could rout an army like the mob he had seen. Tai Cheong said that someone should organize and discipline an army, so that China might hold her own against foreign aggressors and be able to dethrone the Manchus. Then Ho Tung said: "Who knows but that you were born to be the new Napoleon for China?"[1]

In their talks the Taiping Rebellion was discussed, and the fact that it had its beginnings in the destruction of idols no doubt influenced the two friends to perform a really extraordinary and daring deed, which led to important results.

Animated by the spirit of rebellion against ancient superstitions, the two youths invited a few companions to accompany them to the village temple at a time when its guardian would be absent. There, at one end, were the three chief idols, the one in the center being Buck Dai, the god to whose service Tai Cheong had been dedicated by his mother. This god had the finger of one hand upraised, while in the other he grasped a sword. In order to show defiance of this god and of

[1] Statement of Luke Chan, the nephew of Luke Ho Tung.

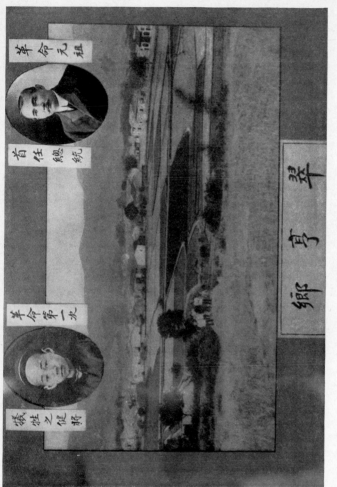

## CHOY HUNG

### THE VILLAGE WHERE SUN YAT SEN WAS BORN

The inscription in Chinese with the picture of Dr. Sun, to the right, describes him as the first President of China and the leader of the revolution. The picture to the left shows his friend, Luke Ho Tung, as a small boy, with an inscription describing him as a first martyr for the cause of the revolution; he was beheaded in 1895.

idolatry in general, Tai Cheong, the leader, went to the idol and broke off the upraised finger; he also tried to twist off the head, but only succeeded in partly turning it.

Then he went to the goddess on the left, and with his knife scraped off the paint from her face. Her name was Keum Fah, the goddess of flowers, to whom was committed the care of children. Some alarm being given, the goddess on the right, Tin Hau, the queen of Heaven, was not molested.

Of course the news of this outrage spread through the village like wildfire, and the people, young and old, flocked to see what had been done. Luke Chan, who tells the story, then a boy, was there with the crowd and looked on in horror. Readers who have watched an excited Chinese crowd can imagine the scene, and the loud talking of the men and women. The chief emotion of the villagers was fear. Their gods had been defied; the beings to whom they looked for protection had been insulted. They believed this act would bring evil and perhaps disaster to the place unless reparation was made at once. The father must pay the cost of repairs, and at a council of the elders it was decided that the young man must leave the village immediately; then perhaps the anger of the gods would be appeased.

Considering all the circumstances, the courage and daring of Tai Cheong can hardly be overestimated. He defied the authority of his father and showed his contempt for the system of idolatry, which ran through the whole social structure. More than this, he seemed to have aimed a blow at the entire Celestial Kingdom. This was what western learning had done for the son of Sun Tat Sung!

It was not a deed committed on the impulse of the moment; it had been talked over and deliberately planned. Tai Cheong knew the danger to himself which would follow. He had witnesses to the act, but he was its sole perpetrator. It was a demonstration that he put truth and conscience above any authority on earth and believed that the all-powerful God was on his side.

Tai Cheong and his friend, Luke Ho Tung, were evidently rebels at heart; and it is not too much to say that the first act of the revolution which he later planned, occurred in the temple at Choy Hung. In support of this, shortly before his death, Sun Yat Sen wrote that the revolution began in 1885, the year in which he defied the idols.

The elders of the village had decreed that Tai Cheong must leave the place, so at nineteen years of age he went from the home of his fathers, not knowing what was before him. He knew no one of his own race in China to whom he could go for sympathy and aid. He made up his mind to go to Canton where there were Christian missions.

Tai Cheong, soon to be called Sun Yat Sen, had commenced a career of revolt which was eventually to convulse the whole of China and to affect the interests and policies of the whole civilized world.

## CHAPTER IV

# Tai Cheong Becomes Sun Yat Sen

### He Studies Medicine in Hongkong, and Takes a New Symbolic Name. He Is Baptized. He Becomes a Revolutionist

WHEN Tai Cheong left Choy Hung he had to walk about a mile and a half to the landing place for junks which plied on the estuary of the Pearl River, really a small inland sea. On its shores are many villages, and innumerable junks carry passengers and freight to any point for which they may be hired. For a few cash[1] he could readily obtain passage to Canton.

There were a number of Christian mission stations in the ancient capital of Kwangtung Province, and Tai Cheong set out to find one of them. Before long he saw a foreigner come from a building; and, going up to him, he said, "Good morning, sir." The man to whom he spoke, Dr. John L. Kerr, who was connected with the Anglo-American Hospital, a mission institution, was surprised to be addressed in good English by a Chinese, for few of that race spoke the language in Canton at that time. He invited the youth into his office and questioned him, asking him what school he had attended. What Tai Cheong thought best to tell the doctor is not known, but it is evident that with his accustomed reti-

---

[1] Cash, the name of the smallest Chinese coin.

cence he told but little. From what the doctor said later it is certain that he did not know the boy had been in Honolulu, neither did he know about the escapade in the temple at Choy Hung.

The result of the conversation was that Dr. Kerr thought it would be valuable for the institution to have a young Chinese who knew English so well, and he made him an offer to enter the service of the hospital as an orderly. He remained there for about a year, commending himself by his intelligence, his studiousness, and his attention to his duties. He had in the performance of his work an opportunity of observing the benefits of the modern way of caring for the sick, which he compared in his mind with the practice of the old style doctors in Choy Hung and with the superstitions about diseases and their cures. He knew the strange things in the *materia medica* used by the Chinese doctors and their lack of surgical ability.

The result of living in such an environment led him to wish to study medicine and surgery in the modern scientific way. Fortunately, at this time there was a plan under discussion for the establishment of a medical school for Chinese students. Dr. Kerr, being informed of his desire, told him that this institution was soon to be opened in Hongkong by a missionary society.

While in Canton, Tai Cheong kept in touch with his family, and, in 1886, being now twenty years old he was told that it was time for him to marry. The marriage was of course arranged, according to Chinese custom, by the parents. They selected a young woman of a neighboring village whose name was Lu Szu, a Punti with little bound feet. Neither of the contracting parties saw each other until the bride lifted her veil during the ceremony, but they expected nothing else and were quite content. The bridegroom returned to Canton and the wife remained with her mother-in-law to serve her as sons' wives generally did.

At marriage Sun Tai Cheong was given his married name, Tuck Mung, the characters for which mean "illustrious virtue." He was never called by this name but it was added to the family scroll, as were the other names which he afterward assumed or which were given to him. He did not remain in Canton long, but went to Hongkong and spent his time in preparatory studies until the day when the medical school should open.

While at Hongkong he was under Christian influence and was instructed for baptism by Mr. Hagar of the American Congregational Mission. He had a friend who was prepared at the same time and was baptized at the same service. This young man was Tong Phong, who went to the United States as a merchant and for years had a business in New York. He is now president of the Chinese-American Bank in Honolulu.

Meanwhile, plans for the medical school progressed favorably; and in June, 1887, Dr. James Cantlie came out from England to open the College of Medicine for Chinese students in October. He met with encouragement from several prominent physicians who believed that there should be Chinese doctors to supply a great need. The classes were held in the Alice Memorial Hospital, which had been founded by a Chinese named Ho Kai, who had studied in the University of Edinburgh and had become a barrister-at-law. He married an Englishwoman and after her death founded this hospital and gave it her name as a memorial. He was afterward knighted, becoming Sir Ho Kai. The College of Medicine was later merged in the University of Hongkong.

Dr. Cantlie was eminent in his profession and took great interest in Tai Cheong, to whom he always refers in his writing as Sun, using the family name. It is evident from what Dr. Cantlie wrote of Sun that he knew little of his history prior to his becoming a student under him. In his book, *Sun Yat Sen and the Awakening of China*, he shows that he did not know where Sun was born or that he had attended school in Hawaii, and that he believed his father was a Christian. It is probable that the doctor made little inquiry about his past, and had little to do with him outside of the classroom. The British in Hongkong meet Chinese in business but have no social relations with them, and this aloofness no doubt accounts for the doctor's lack of information.

As a student Tai Cheong won the good opinion of those who were over him, as being painstaking and capable. He made few friends, for he devoted all his time to work; and yet he was thinking of China, its government, and the need of the people for enlightenment. His old school friend, C. K. Ai, made a visit to Hongkong at this time and they took long walks together in the evenings, until the hour of nine when, at that period, by ordinance, all Chinese had to be indoors. On these occasions he talked freely about conditions in China, and compared the opportunities which the Chinese had in Honolulu and other countries with those they had in their own country.

This was the first time C. K. Ai had ever heard him give expression to such opinions, and later when Sun was engaged in insurrections he recalled the conversations as showing that Sun was then thinking along lines which led him to become a rebel. Tai Cheong was grieved that the French could so easily annex Indo-China, because China with its millions of people had no modern army or navy. He did not tell his friend of any plans, but he did emphasize the need of modern education. He said he had been reading books and was dissatisfied with the system of government under the Manchus, which had been suited for China in the past but now kept her back from taking the place in the world which she ought to have.

Sun was the first graduate of the Hongkong School of Medicine, and in 1892 he received his diploma which authorized him to practice medicine and surgery. He decided to open an office in Macao, the Portuguese colony, situated across the bay about forty miles from Hongkong. It was at this time that he assumed the name of Sun Yat Sen, by which he has been generally known to the world. The many names that a Chinese may possess are often a puzzle to a foreigner. Sun Tai Cheong now became Sun Yat Sen.

The meaning of the name is of interest. The characters representing Yat and Sen are found in poetry. Yat means unconventional, or free. Sen means a genie or spirit. To a Chinese scholar the two characters convey the idea that he was as free as a spirit, that is, free from the old conventional Chinese medical methods. Others interpret the characters to mean that he was now free to exercise magical powers as a genie.

When he became a revolutionist he changed the characters so that they meant something quite different, though the sounds would be spelled by the same letters in English. With the new characters, Yat would mean literally, daily, and Sen, renovation—the whole significance being that the day for the renovation of China had arrived. When the followers of Dr. Sun write his name they always use the last adopted pair of characters.

Macao was founded by the Portuguese in 1557, but its trade was much restricted until the five treaty ports were opened to foreigners in 1842. In 1892 it was notorious for deriving its revenue chiefly from the licensing of gambling houses. There was a Chinese hospital there in which the old style of medicine was practiced. But permission was granted to Dr. Sun to try his foreign methods, and of this he at once took advantage. His chief work here was surgery, and several times when he had to perform a serious operation Dr. Cantlie came over to assist his promising pupil. He said there was something in the personality of Sun which attracted men to him and made them glad to help him.[1]

Dr. Sun did not remain long in Macao, for the law of the colony permitted only those who had a Portuguese diploma to practice modern medicine. Chinese of the old school were not interfered with, but Dr. Sun was not of that kind and he would draw business away from the Portuguese. So he was given notice that he must cease practicing there.

Although Dr. Sun's stay in Macao was short, something most important occurred there which changed the current of his life. He met men who had formed a society called "Young China." In Macao men were free to talk of the evils existing in their country. They met and discussed the graft and corruption of the officials; this they believed was largely due to the small salaries

[1] Cantlie, *Sun Yat Sen and the Awakening of China.*

they received, which they were expected to augment by the system of "squeeze" prevailing all along the line from the highest to the lowest representative of the government. This movement was not political, and those engaged in it advocated a peaceful reformation to be brought about by education, petition, and agitation.

The principles of this progressive group found soil ready to receive and develop them, when they reached the mind and heart of Sun Yat Sen. His life in Honolulu and Hongkong had already led him to think deeply on these lines, as we have seen. Here was an organization intended to advance the ideas which for some time he had held. No people in the world are more given to forming societies than the Chinese, and such organizations had in the past often had a powerful influence in the remedying of evils, both locally and even in Peking. The guilds in Canton were very powerful; they had frequently protested against extortions of various kinds, and although they were viewed with suspicion, they were feared and heed was paid to their petitions.

This Society of Young China wished to extend the democratic principle of government existing in the villages, so that the people might have some voice in provincial and national affairs. The first thing they had in mind was education on modern lines. They valued the classics; but they knew that the educated man, according to Chinese standards, while learned in the classics, knew nothing of the world or of modern science. They burned with zeal to do their part in bringing China out of its stagnation—a task which was impossible under the old system.

Most of the young men who took part in this progressive movement, and in the first attempt at revolution, had been educated in mission schools. Americans and British had missions in Kwangtung, and there were also the Basle and the Berlin missions. While the missions did not purposely teach anything hostile to the government, yet their teaching inevitably led to a spirit of revolt against injustice and wrong. When the young men and women were freed from the fear of evil spirits and the wrath of the gods, their minds were open to see the evils of ignorance, fraud, and cruelty.

With his heart stirred by association with the men of Young China, Sun Yat Sen went to Canton and there found his friend, Luke Ho Tung, who had been with him in Choy Hung when he had mutilated the gods. He was quite ready to join in any movement which had for its object the improvement of conditions in China. Secret meetings were held by those in sympathy with them, and plans of procedure were discussed. They were convinced that the first step to take was to endeavor to bring about a reform in the system of education. They decided that the best way to accomplish this was to get the guilds of Canton interested, and these were quietly approached to see whether any assistance could be obtained from them.

These guilds were of ancient origin and their rules were a law to their members. They were democratic and rendered protection and aid to members when they got into trouble. Years before Captain Boycott had given his name to a coercive method in Ireland, the guilds had used it, and it had served their purpose well. Their protests had been heeded by viceroys and even by Peking.

The plan of Dr. Sun and his associates was to get the guilds to petition the Manchu government to inaugurate a change in educational methods, and as an opening wedge, to ask for the establishment of agricultural schools that the people might be taught better ways than their primitive style of farming. But the guilds were conservative, they could not be brought to see the advantages of foreign methods, as advocated by men who had come under the influence of white foreigners. Besides they were not seeking trouble and knew that any suggestion of changes made to the Manchu government would be likely to lead the authorities at Peking to imagine that the Cantonese, who had often given them trouble, were trying to get something which would upset the existing order. They declined to have anything to do with the matter.

The young progressive party was disappointed but not dismayed. They at once organized what they called "The Educational Society," the name in their judgment avoiding all appearance of a political movement. Of this society Dr. Sun was the acknowledged head. He had foreign learning and experience, and a natural capacity for leadership, so he now came to the fore, a position which he retained until his death.

The bold young men decided to petition the Peking government, setting forth the desirability of establishing agricultural schools and pointing out the advantages of improving the condition of the farmers through the variation and increase in crops. The document was couched in literary language in the most approved form, and avoided any references to grievances. Dr. Sun appended his name, not Sun Yat Sen but a new name, Sun Wen, and by this he was always known at Peking and by those with whom he had formal communication. It became in fact his official name which he signed to all documents, including his will, made during his last illness.

Wen is the Mandarin pronunciation of the character and it represents the idea of literacy. It is the term which appears in Wen Li, which means the literary language as used by scholars. In the Punti it is Wun, and in Hakka, Mun, but of course the character is identical in each case. Sun Wen meant Sun the Scholar.

Up to this time he had five names, but this does not appear strange to Chinese. The five were, Tai Cheong, his boy name; Tuck Mung, his marriage name, never used; Sun Yat Sen with its two meanings; and Sun Wen, his official appellation.

The petition aroused grave suspicion in Peking. The proposed innovation showed foreign influence, and the feeling against foreigners was strong among the members of the Manchu government. Especially was this the case with the old Dowager Empress, the real ruler; with all her natural ability, she was densely ignorant of the world outside China. The reply was emphatically unfavorable. The old learning had made China great, there was no need of imitating the ways of barbarians whose methods threatened injury to the country.

Peaceful means having failed, and respectful appeals having been rejected with disdain, the Educational Society recognized that if any change was to be made it would have to be brought about by revolution. The members were young men of a class which had no influence; they knew the rigid conservatism pervading all the strata of society; they knew their weakness, and that their numbers were few; but they believed the people

帝象　德明　日新　逸仙　孫文　中山

## THE SIX NAMES OF SUN YAT SEN

In order from the top they are: his boy name; his marriage name; his name as a doctor of medicine; his name as a revolutionist; his official name, the name he generally used after 1895; the name often used now in speaking of him.

could be aroused. They thought the way to arouse them was to accuse the Manchus of being the cause of all the corruption and oppression that existed. The Manchus were usurpers, they were not Chinese. The Cantonese hated the Manchus, and these young men were convinced that if some open act of revolt were staged the people would flock to their standard. They determined to put their belief to the test. It is pitiful to think of them in their poverty and weakness, plotting a revolution.[1]

To those who have read the foregoing story it will be seen that the stand which Dr. Sun now took was the result of gradual development. He was naturally of an independent and determined disposition. His life abroad, his association with foreigners, his reading of books on history and government, all had made him dissatisfied with conditions in China. He was of strong convictions and fearless when questions of his beliefs were concerned. This he had shown when he refused to submit to his older brother in Honolulu and when he defied the gods and incurred the anger of the villagers in Choy Hung. Now when the Manchus had rejected reasonable petitions, the spirit of revolt took possession of him. They were to him the embodiment of injustice and wrong, he would devote his life to accomplish their overthrow.

He knew that many dynasties in China had been overthrown by the uprisings of the people. He had read of the French Revolution and studied the writings of Rousseau. He knew the great gains for freedom and progress which had been brought about by revolutions,

[1] This account of the movement is from the relations of those who took part in it.

and he felt that the only hope for China was the overthrow of the Manchus. So he became a thoroughgoing
revolutionist; and giving up his medical practice, he
threw himself with all his ability into the movement.
As a leader he developed extraordinary qualities and had
the implicit confidence and enthusiastic support of his
associates.

## CHAPTER V

# The First Attempt at Revolution

## The Heroism of Luke Ho Tung.  Sun Yat Sen
## Escapes

INSURRECTIONS have been far from uncommon in China; her annals tell of many attempts at revolution during her long history. Four hundred years before Christ, the sage Mencius taught that "The people are the most important element in a country." In this saying lie the seeds of democracy, for Mencius held that the principle extended to all its consequences.

Sun Yat Sen and his companions knew well that a latent spirit of rebellion existed in the hearts of the Cantonese; and in their enthusiasm believed that if a blow were struck this would at once show itself. So the meeting place of the Educational Society became the headquarters of the plotters of a revolution. They were familiar with the story of the Taiping Rebellion, and knew how the people had eagerly followed the leaders when they announced their slogan, "Down with the Manchus." They knew how nearly successful that rebellion had been and they believed it would have been victorious if the Emperor had not called in foreign aid.

The movement under Dr. Sun had only one thing in common with that of the Taipings—the hatred of the Manchus. The story of that uprising throws some light on the readiness of the Cantonese to rebel. In a village thirty miles from Canton was born Hung Siu Tsuen, the originator of the Taiping movement. He became despondent, and for a time insane, when he failed to get his literary degree. While out of his mind he said he was the King of Heaven. He had been reading tracts given him by a missionary and when he recovered he believed they explained his visions. He and a companion baptized each other and soon had a hundred followers. In 1846 he organized the Society of God Worshipers, and in a year there were two thousand members. These converts went from village to village destroying idols, until they were arrested. Some of them experienced extraordinary ecstatic fits; some spoke in strange tongues; others issued edicts in the name of the Heavenly Father and of the Elder Brother Jesus. Hung Siu Tsuen was proclaimed the Holy Spirit. At first some of the missionaries favored the movement, but later its excesses alienated them. It soon assumed enormous proportions and became an organized rebellion against the Manchus. The rebels marched from place to place, and in 1853 took Nanking and began a march on Peking. Trade at Shanghai and Canton being greatly interfered with, the British decided to assist the government in putting down the rebellion, and for this purpose gave the services of Capt. Charles Gordon. Several million persons were estimated to have lost their lives in the campaigns. Taiping means Great Peace, and the belief of the rebels was that if the Manchus were destroyed, the Kingdom of Heaven would be established on earth with Hung Siu Tsuen as king.

Sun Yat Sen saw the disadvantages of advocating revolt openly, and realized that secrecy in organization and propaganda was essential. A few trusted men were admitted into the society, and a plan was formulated to procure arms and overthrow the guards of the yamen, the headquarters of the Mandarin government. It was believed that these guards could easily be overcome, and then the arms and ammunition stored on the premises would be at the service of the revolutionary party. They felt sure that with this initial success multitudes would join them, and soon the whole province of Kwangtung would be in their hands.

To purchase arms money was required, and in this Luke Ho Tung, who was with the conspirators heart and soul, was of great assistance. He had some land in Choy Hung which he sold, putting all the proceeds into the treasury of the society. He also sold his wife's jewels and gave this money to the fund. Others gave what they could, and the Chinese often give freely when they espouse a cause.

The petition which had been sent to Peking had aroused suspicion, and the authorities had spies watching those who had signed it. Despite this, the plotters obtained a quantity of small arms and ammunition from Hongkong, which they stored at the headquarters of the Educational Society. These supplies had come in barrels marked "English mud," which is the Chinese name for cement. They also laid in several pairs of scissors with which they intended to cut off the cues of the revolutionists after the first success, in order to show that they were free from the Manchu yoke, for this style of wearing the hair had been imposed on the Chinese as a mark of subjection to the Manchus.

In October, 1895, the plans for the uprising were completed, when an informer told the authorities that there was a revolutionary movement on foot and designated the place where the arms were stored. At first it was not believed, but spies were sent out and they reported that the information was correct. It was Luke Ho Tung who suspected that there was danger; and fearing the headquarters would be raided, urged Sun Yat Sen, as the leader, to try to leave Canton immediately. It was arranged that Luke Ho Tung and a few volunteers would remain at headquarters and burn all incriminating papers, and, if they had time, conceal the arms. The papers must be destroyed first in order to save the lives of those implicated in the plot, whose names appeared on the lists.

Dr. Sun left the house, but before Luke Ho Tung and his companions could finish their task, the officers came and arrested the five brave men still remaining, who had sacrificed themselves to save their leader and others.

Sun Yat Sen escaped, and after difficulties reached Hongkong. The five who were taken were cast into a loathsome jail where criminals and political prisoners were confined. There they were treated without mercy, and as plotters against the government their condition was worse than that of thieves and murderers. Luke Ho Tung being an avowed Christian, some of that faith sent a petition to the authorities pleading for a mitigation of the penalty of death, and gave it to be understood that they were ready to back this request with the usual gifts expected in such cases. But the offense was too serious and if the request were granted there would be embarrassing inquiries from Peking.

In this plea for mercy Luke Ho Tung would have no part, as he would ask no favors of the Manchus. When the petition was denied he issued a statement which was called his confession, in which he dwelt upon the

wrongs which China had suffered, and the policy of the
Peking government in holding the country back by its
refusal to favor any step leading to the enlightenment
of the people.

Luke Ho Tung and three of his companions were
taken to the execution grounds and beheaded, the fifth
man having already died in prison. If Luke Ho Tung
had lived he would have been one of the chief men of
the revolutionary party, for he was not only an excellent
Chinese scholar and familiar with English, but brave
and devoted to the movement. He was one of the first
martyrs for the cause, and his name should be so
honored. As in other cases, the blood of the martyrs
was the seed from which multitudes sprang up to work,
and if necessary to die for the enlightenment of China.[1]
Many years later Dr. Sun wrote in the highest terms of
this young man who had been his friend and associate.

The great-uncle of Luke Ho Tung was at that time
the head elder at Choy Hung; and as such he was afraid
he would get into trouble as responsible, according to
Chinese custom, for the conduct of one of the villagers.
He escaped, but another relative, the father of Luke
Chan of Honolulu, was cast into prison. He had been
successful in business and Dr. Sun had consulted him,
but he had had no part in the uprising. His house of
confinement at Canton was a place of horror, the food
was poor and meager, and the lack of sanitary arrangements made it very unhealthy. The first year he suffered
greatly, but when the officials learned that he was an
excellent Chinese scholar, he was given clerical work
and better treatment. His son, in Honolulu, tried in

[1] Luke Chan, the nephew of Luke Ho Tung, gave the foregoing
information.

every way possible to procure his release and spent, first and last, some six thousand dollars in getting up petitions and seeing that influential people presented them. Finally he sent a petition to Minister Wu Ting Fang who then represented China in Washington. This was written in the most approved style, and stated that the man had done no wrong, that he had been in prison six years, and there was no one at home to care for his feeble wife. It was through Minister Wu's influence that the prisoner was released. If he had not been able to make himself useful, he would no doubt have died as many others did in the prison during his stay there.

This story illustrates the fear in which lived those who were suspected of aiding Sun Yat Sen.

It will have been noted that Dr. Sun, and some of the men associated with him, were Christians. This led to the opinion that the foreign religion made men rebellious. The opinion was based on fact, for wherever Christianity has been preached it has made men dissatisfied with wrong and tyranny. This is the accusation made against Christian missions everywhere, and it has truth on its side—for the religion of Jesus teaches the worth of the individual and this leads to the turning upside down of many old customs. While the social structure of China had many excellent points, there was so much cruelty and oppression in the political life of the nation that young Chinese who had been educated in mission schools developed a burning hatred toward the whole system.

It has been said that Dr. Sun, in later life, drifted away from the Christian faith, chiefly because he did not emphasize it. The fact is, he had to deal with men as he found them and most of his followers were Con-

fucianists. To alienate these would have ruined the
cause. He had tact and common sense enough to avoid
doing so, and advocated principles which they could
understand and which would move them to action. He
understood the common people and appealed to them
as one of themselves.

After his escape from Canton, Dr. Sun remained in
Hongkong for a short time, secreted by friends. He
knew that spies were on the watch for him, and a large
reward offered for his capture. He was afraid he might
be kidnapped and carried to Canton. Consulting a
lawyer to learn whether he would have any protection
from the British authorities, he learned that charges
would be brought against him if he were found and he
would probably be handed over to the Chinese officials.
He was advised that the wise thing to do was to leave
the city as soon as possible.

Dr. Sun determined to go to Kobe, and friends in
Hongkong, where he had many sympathizers, provided
him with funds. In March, 1895, after the brief war
between Japan and China, peace had been made; so he
could go to Kobe. In that war Japan had demonstrated
that an oriental country which had adopted modern
ways could easily defeat undisciplined forces, and this
only made him more anxious for a change in China.

When he reached Kobe he was not safe, for the principle of extraterritoriality was in force in Japan until
1899, and if he had been arrested he would have been
taken before the Chinese Consul and deported.

Knowledge of this, no doubt, was partly instrumental
in leading him to take a step which was of great significance. He cut off his cue, so that he could dress like
a Japanese and pass as one. The act also served to show

that he had renounced allegiance to the Manchus. In 1896, he wrote the following account for an English magazine:

I cut off my cue which I had worn all my life. For some days I had not shaved my head, and I allowed the hair on my upper lip to grow. Then I went to a clothier and bought a suit of modern Japanese garments. When I was fully dressed I looked in a mirror, and was astonished, and a great deal assured by the transformation. Nature favored me, for I was darker in complexion than most Chinese, a trait I had inherited from my mother. I have seen it stated that I had Malay blood, and also that I was born in Honolulu, both these statements are false. I am purely Chinese, but after the Japanese war, when the Japanese began to be treated with more respect, I had no trouble in passing for a Japanese. I admit I owe a great deal to this circumstance, as otherwise I should not have escaped many dangerous situations.[1]

As we have seen, the mother, wife, and children of Dr. Sun had gone to Hawaii for safety. They were now with his brother, Ah Mi, and he resolved to follow them. He felt that he could arouse an interest among his countrymen there, and he had it in mind to go to the United States where he hoped to get sympathy and financial aid.

[1] The *Strand Magazine*.

## CHAPTER VI

# In Honolulu, the United States, and England

## Sun's Escape from Captivity in the Chinese Legation in London

S UN YAT SEN reached Honolulu early in 1896. He was no stranger there and had friends with whom he could stay. The Chinese in Hawaii were all Cantonese, and they had been kept informed of the revolutionary movement in Canton. Their life in the Islands had been such that they were ready to appreciate the principles for which Dr. Sun was fighting. Nowhere in the world are the Chinese as progressive as in Hawaii, where they have been treated fairly and where their children have been allowed to attend the public schools. They are respected for their industry and integrity, and the white people feel kindly toward them. Dr. Sun soon began to gather a few men together and discuss his business with them.

He had not been long in Honolulu when his old friend and teacher, Dr. James Cantlie, passed through on his way to England. As the ship was to be a day in port, Dr. Cantlie engaged a carriage for a drive about the city, taking with him his wife and her Japanese maid. As they were going along a man called to them from the sidewalk, and came out to the carriage. He was taken for a Japanese, and the doctor had the Japanese woman speak to him. The man was Sun, who spoke to them in English, but even then he was not recognized, so he told them who he was. Of course they had much to talk about, and at parting the doctor invited Sun to stay with him when he reached England. Sun's disguise certainly was effective; Dr. Cantlie wrote, "He had no cue, had grown a mustache, and was dressed in European clothes."[1]

Dr. Sun spent some months in Honolulu and was busy speaking in private and in public, making converts for his cause. When he thought the time was ripe he called a meeting at the house of a friend, Ho Fon, at which about thirty were present. After explanation and discussion it was decided to form an organization and to call it Hung Chung Hui, which means "The Progressive Chinese Society." Each one who was admitted had to take an oath that he would be faithful and true to the cause; that he would not reveal the secret purposes of the society; that he would respond to the call of the leader for service; and that he would work for the revolution and aid it with his gifts according to his ability.

A number of men who were present at that meeting are known to the writer, being still residents of Honolulu. The secretary is still living, but the records were destroyed in the fire in Honolulu in 1900, which wiped out the Chinese district. Their chief adviser was Li Chung, who had been brought from China by the Hawaiian Government to act as court interpreter. He had been educated in Queen's College, Hongkong, and was a valuable addition to the membership. He administered the oaths to the members, the first man to be sworn being Sun Yat Sen who, placing his left hand on an

[1] Cantlie, *Sun Yat Sen*.

open Bible and raising his right toward heaven, called God to witness his sincerity. One by one those present followed his example, knowing that it might mean for them danger or even death. They were all young men, some not out of their teens. A number of them are prominent in business today, as merchants, bankers, or employees in large wholesale houses in Honolulu.

The next meeting of the society was held at a place which would accommodate a larger number of men, and on this occasion about one hundred were present. At a third meeting there were many more. All were full of enthusiasm. As they knew there would be fighting, it was decided that the men ought to have some military drill; and a Dane, Victor Bache, who had been in the army, was engaged to instruct them. W. Yap was chosen captain, and C. K. Ai, lieutenant. They met for drill in the yard of the Rev. Frank Damon, who was in charge of the Chinese mission work in Hawaii but was not in the secrets of the society. The young men met twice a week and used sticks in practicing the manual of arms.

During his stay in Honolulu Dr. Sun collected about $6,000, which was a very large sum in those days, for most of the Chinese were in very moderate circumstances. Later some of the Chinese in Honolulu and elsewhere gave all the money they had saved to the cause. Dr. Sun left Honolulu in June, 1896, and then stated that he believed nine-tenths of his countrymen in the Islands were with him. He sailed for San Francisco where he received a warm welcome among the many Chinese there, and secured generous contributions. From that city he went to various places in the United States where there were Chinese, and everywhere enlisted men in the movement. Practically all the Chinese in the United States were Cantonese and traditional haters of the Manchus.

Everywhere Dr. Sun made the same appeal, and when he told the people that they were striving to make China a republic they were enthusiastic. He said the change could only be made by a revolution such as had occurred in America when it became free from the rule of Great Britain. They were living in a republic, where their lives and property were safe, and the word republic appealed to them.

While in America Sun heard that the Chinese Minister in Washington was doing his best to have him kidnapped with a view of having him shipped back to China. He knew the fate which would await him if he were caught and taken back, of which he wrote:

First having my ankles crushed in a vise and broken by a hammer, my eyelids cut off, and finally being chopped to small fragments, so that none could claim my mortal remains. For the old Chinese code does not err on the side of mercy to political offenders.

He sailed from New York for England in September, 1896, and on reaching London became a guest of Dr. Cantlie. What he expected to accomplish in England is not clear. There were few Chinese in the country, but he may have thought that he might interest some kindly disposed persons to aid in liberating China by making a loan payable when the republic of China should be declared, as we know he did on a later visit. He knew from his reading that Englishmen had been sympathetic with the Poles, the Hungarians, and others in their struggle for freedom, and that he might find some who would be interested in freeing the millions in China.

It is known that he wished to ascertain whether he could make arrangements for the purchase of arms. He had some money, and he was going to Singapore and the Straits Settlements, where there were many thousands of his countrymen, some of them rich; there he might obtain funds for munitions.

He had been very shrewd in avoiding spies so far, and he had always booked passage under assumed names, but he felt safe in England. Danger, however, followed him there; on Sunday, October 11, he was caught. Here is his story in his own words:

I was walking down Devonshire Street on my way to church, when a Chinese met me and asked whether I was a Chinese or a Japanese. I told him, and he said he was a Cantonese too. Conversing in Punti as we walked along we met another Chinese. They pressed me to go to their lodging and have a smoke. I demurred as I said I was to meet Dr. Cantlie at church. We met another Chinese and the first one left us. When we were near the door of a house, which door was open, one on each side compelled me to enter the house. I suspected nothing but when I was inside the door was shut and locked, all at once it flashed over me that I was in the Chinese Legation.

The Legation people had been informed from Washington and they had been watching for me. They sent to Dr. Cantlie's house for my papers, but he would not give them up in my absence, and if they had received them, there would have been many executions in China for all the names of the Society were on them. Sir Halliday McCartney was my chief inquisitor and he told me that a berth had been engaged to take me to China and that I was to be hidden until the ship sailed.

I was locked in a room under strict surveillance for twelve days, awaiting my transportation on board ship, as a lunatic, back to China, and I should never have escaped, had not my old friend, Dr. Cantlie, been then living in London. To him I managed after many failures to get through a message.

Sir Halliday McCartney was the English Secretary of the Legation.

Dr. Sun tried throwing messages, weighted with money, out of the window. One of them was picked up by a legation servant and then the windows were nailed up. In his desperation he managed to bribe an English servant to carry a message to Dr. Cantlie.

As usual a woman came to the rescue. The wife of one of the English servants in the Legation heard from her husband the piteous plight of the imprisoned Chinese and sent Dr. Cantlie the following letter:

There is a friend of yours imprisoned in the Chinese lega-tion here since last Sunday. They intend to send him back to China, where it is certain they will hang him. It is very sad for the poor man and unless something is done at once he will be taken away and no one will know it. I dare not sign my name, but this is the truth, so believe what I say. Whatever you do must be done at once, or it will be too late. His name is, I believe, Sin Yin Sen.

The note was left at Dr. Cantlie's door at 11.30 P.M. on October 17. The doorbell rang and the doctor got out of bed, went downstairs, and found the letter pushed under the door, the person who placed it there having gone. He went at once to Scotland Yard and the headman told him it was none of his business. He went again the next day but they would pay no attention to his story, telling him he was crazy. The doctor was nearly frantic for there was no time to lose. He went to the Foreign Office where he knew an official.[1] This friend at once took the matter up and carried it to Lord Salisbury, who assisted in the release of the prisoner. If

[1] Cantlie, *Sun Yat Sen.*

this had not been done, twenty hours later, Sun Yat Sen would have been on a vessel bound for China, where like some of his followers he would have suffered death. The British could not enter the Legation building and release the prisoner, but they so hedged it about with detectives and policemen that he could not be smuggled out to a steamer. Finally, seeing the futility of holding him longer, the Chinese Minister let him go.

Of all his escapes, and he had many, none were so narrow as this one. The English newspapers had long accounts of the affair and from that day Dr. Sun Yat Sen was known all over the English-speaking world. He gained more than publicity through being kidnapped— the sympathy of a very large number of people who had the methods and practices of the Manchu government brought vividly before them. He became a hero fighting for liberty, in the eyes of the multitude. But amid all the attention shown him he did not forget to reward the man and his wife who got the message to Dr. Cantlie.

After his escape he wrote to the *London Times* as follows:

Will you kindly express through your columns my keen appreciation of the action of the British Government in effecting my release from the Chinese Legation. I have also to thank the press generally for their timely help and sympathy. If anything were needed to convince me of the generous public spirit which pervades Great Britain, and the love of justice which distinguishes its people, the recent acts of the last few days have conclusively done so.

Knowing and feeling more keenly than ever what a constitutional government and an enlightened people mean, I am prompted to pursue the cause of advancement, education, and civilization, in my own beloved but oppressed country.

Shortly after his release Dr. Sun wrote to his friend, the Rev. F. C. Au of Hongkong, telling him of his imprisonment and escape.

I was captured and confined in the London Legation for over ten days. The Chinese Minister planned to tie me up and send me to a ship at night. A ship for such purpose had been chartered. The Minister only waited for the right moment to take me out of the Legation and put me on board the ship. During the first six or seven days of my confinement nobody knew of this. While in prison, I thought that I should surely meet death and that I could never hope to live again. It is but natural for a person to beseech Heaven in time of need as it is to call one's parents when suffering from pain or trouble. In my case it was true. In those days of suffering, I only beat my heart and repented and earnestly prayed. For six or seven days I prayed incessantly day and night. The more I prayed the more earnest I was in my prayer. On the seventh day, I felt suddenly comforted. I was absolutely without fear. I never made any attempt to put myself in that state. The state of being comforted and feeling brave came to me unconsciously. This was the result of prayer. How fortunate I was to have received the Grace of God. . . .[1]

The remainder of the letter tells how he escaped. Afterward Dr. Sun spent some time at the home of Dr. Cantlie, who comments on the fact that Sun was always studying constitutional history, and everything that would help him in the work to which he had dedicated his life. His travels in the United States and England, the people whom he met, the material progress which he observed, the liberty under law which prevailed, all contributed to prepare him better for what he preached and what he hoped to achieve.

[1] Translated by Professor Shao Chang Lee from a Hongkong paper.

## CHAPTER VII

# Travels

## Sun's Work of Preparation for the Insurrection of 1900

ON leaving London, Sun Yat Sen went to Paris where he made a brief stay, and then spent a short time in visiting places of interest in Europe. But his real business was in the Orient, and he soon sailed for Singapore. His fame had, of course, preceded him and he was well received by his countrymen, who constituted a large proportion of the population of that city and of the Straits Settlements generally. Some of these were wealthy but he did personal work among the rich and poor alike, as well as making public addresses, everywhere presenting in his forceful manner the idea that the only way to bring about progress and enlightenment in China was by a revolution which should put an end to the rule of the Manchus.

With his singular persuasiveness and his wide knowledge of affairs, he enlisted hosts of recruits, and organized these as he had in various other places where he had been. Men trusted him here, as they did everywhere, and made large gifts for the cause. Singapore became one of the strongholds of the revolutionary party and Dr. Sun visited the place on several occasions when in need of funds or when he sought refuge from his enemies. His followers at Singapore did not expect a speedy accomplishment of his purpose. But the Chinese are a tenacious people and when committed to an idea, their patience, persistency, and determination are wonderful. They knew well that before a republic could be established in China much preparatory work would have to be done; that the vast population could not be reached in a hurry; and that even in the province of Kwangtung, whose inhabitants would be most receptive to the message, it might be years before the hour to strike should arrive.

Dr. Sun was in constant communication with the local societies, widely scattered as they were. They were acting under his general directions and were kept informed of the progress which was being made. He saw that as soon as extraterritoriality was abolished in Japan (and he knew that the Powers were taking steps in that direction), there must be headquarters in that country. Although the time for that was not yet come, he decided to go to Japan where there were now many Chinese, especially in Yokohama and in Tokyo. In Tokyo there were a large number of students and he had an idea, which he later carried out, that some of these might study chemistry and be able to make explosives for the revolutionists. On reaching Japan he secretly met groups of his countrymen and talked of China and its needs.

It is remarkable that of the many who were associated with him so few were unfaithful to the trust reposed in them. He speaks on one occasion of some who had failed, but without bitterness, and in only one instance mentions a name. It appears that in Japan he intrusted the funds he had collected to purchase arms to a man named Nakimura who swindled him, so that an empty treasury was faced. It must have been difficult to explain to the Chinese at Singapore that he had been cheated by a Japanese and needed them to contribute generously again, but he returned to that port and evidently got more money.

From Singapore he went back to China where he traveled from place to place under various disguises; sometimes as a coolie, then as a peddler, and again as a Japanese. With a large reward on his head, how he escaped arrest is a marvel; but in the tea houses and in private dwellings he talked of the needs of education and—when it was wise—of the wrongs due to the Manchus. Only to a chosen few did he reveal his identity, and here and there formed a nucleus for future organization into groups, ready to respond to his call.

As this is the story of Sun Yat Sen and of the insurrections in which he took a personal part, many sporadic uprisings cannot be described. These were generally ill timed, but they served the purpose of keeping unrest alive and showed the growing consciousness that reforms must be made.

The war with Japan in 1894–95 and the consequences of defeat, in the forced payment of indemnity and the cession of territory, were followed by demands for concessions to foreign Powers. Thoughtful Chinese saw plainly that changes must take place in methods of education and measures of defense, or there would be danger of the partition of China.

Even before the Japanese war, progressive thinkers had written on the subject of the need of the adoption of western learning and principles of government. Two missionaries, Y. J. Allen and Timothy Richard, had written articles pointing out the progress Japan had made. Several of the Mandarins, including Li Hung

Chang, realized the necessity of reforms. The reformers had frequent consultations with the missionaries.

Kang Yu Wei, a fine scholar who had seen the advantages of modern civilization at Hongkong and Shanghai, wrote a book on the subject which was widely read all over China. Various organizations sent memorials to Peking, respectfully begging that reforms be made. The young Emperor, Kuang Hsu, was impressed with what he read and sent for Kang Yu Wei to come to Peking. It is said that the Emperor's interest was first aroused by reading the beautiful copy of the Bible which ten thousand Christian Chinese women had presented to the old Empress.

The result was that Kuang Hsu determined to inaugurate a number of reforms and in September, 1898, began to issue edicts ordering changes. These related to all departments of government. The system of confining the public examinations wholly to the Chinese classics was abolished. Western learning was to be encouraged as was also foreign travel. Colleges were to be established, the army was to be organized on modern lines, and a new ministry was to be formed.

Sir Robert Hart, who had done so much for China in organizing and managing the customs with an efficiency and honesty which had won for him widespread admiration, when he read the edicts, said: "I never expected to see this." But he and others saw there was too much haste, for what had been attempted in a few months should have been carried out over a long term of years.

The reformers knew that if their plans were to be carried out they must get rid of the Dowager Empress, so they plotted to seize and confine her. Yuan Shih Kai knew of this plot and disclosed it. The Empress and her advisers were violently opposed to the contemplated changes. The old order had made China great and there was no need of copying the methods of the barbarians. She at once went to the capital with an armed force. The Emperor was taken and confined in a wing of the palace, a number of the leaders of the reform movement were taken, seven young men were beheaded, and all officials connected with the movement were degraded.

The Empress was specially anxious to catch Kang Yu Wei, but he fled to Shanghai and there boarded a British steamer for Hongkong. Although he escaped, his relatives were exterminated and the graves of his ancestors destroyed. All the reform edicts were declared null and void.

Discontent with conditions existed not only in the south, it has been shown, but among many leading men all over China. As Dr. Sun was a leading spirit for reform in Kwangtung, he knew he was in danger and thought it best to leave the country. He went again to the United States. In San Francisco he addressed public meetings, both in Chinese and English. At the close of one meeting a young man named Homer Lea came to him and said: "I should like to throw in my lot with you. I believe what you have said and that you will succeed."

Lea was a military enthusiast and Dr. Sun was greatly taken with him; after talking over the situation he made Lea his military adviser. As trained soldiers would be needed for a revolution, plans were made for the formation of bands of Reform Cadets, as they were called, and Lea was appointed general of these organizations. The Chinese youths who joined the cadets in San Francisco were supplied with arms and drilled in halls, and arrangements made for target practice. The idea spread to other cities in the United States; a troop was also formed in Manila. It was reported that before long there were four thousand of these cadets. The Chinese Government was informed of what was taking place and made some effort to stop the activity. It does not appear that any use was made of these cadets in the insurrections which followed in China but individuals did go to the Orient at the call of the leader.

While in San Francisco Dr. Sun was reported to have addressed Americans in these words:

Because you are the pioneers of western civilization in Japan; because you are a Christian nation; because we intend to model our new government after yours; and, above all, because you are the champions of liberty and democracy, we hope to find many Lafayettes among you.

At another time, in referring to the first attempt at rebellion, he said:

It was one of a series which must ultimately triumph in the establishment of a constitutional government in our empire. The whole people of China, except imperialist agents, who profit in purse and power, by the outrages they are able to perpetrate, are with us. The good, well-governed people of America will not fail to understand that the Chinese, numbering many millions in their own land and many thousands in exile, could not entertain such feelings about their empire without cause.

There are no laws as you know law. The people have no voice. There is no appeal, no matter how unjust or cruel. The governors of the provinces grow wealthy by squeezing the people.

Our conspiracy to seize Canton failed. Yet we are filled with hope. Our greatest hope is to make the Bible and Christian education, as we have come to know it in America, the means of conveying to our countrymen what blessings may be in the way of just laws. We intend to try by every means in our power to seize the country and create a government without bloodshed.[1]

If one did not know the facts, he would suppose from such words that the movement which Dr. Sun advocated was a national aspiration rather than the conspiracy of a comparatively small group, composed largely of men who had come under American or European influence. This it certainly was at first, until systematic propaganda and the appeal to the Cantonese hatred of the Manchus aroused the people of the southern province.

Those who know China best do not agree with Sun when he places all the blame for conditions in China on the Manchus. If the system of education was largely responsible for the stagnation of their civilization, the Manchus had found it in operation. That the Chinese scholars knew nothing and cared nothing about the outside world was not the fault of the Manchus.

At times Sun Yat Sen spoke as if the years of the Mings, a Chinese dynasty, were times of peace and good government. He must have known, if he was familiar with history, that the rule of pure Chinese dynasties was often cruel, corrupt, and base. The extraordinary influence of the eunuchs connected with the courts had been a constant danger and source of corruption. The Manchus had deprived them of power.

The popular hatred of the Manchus was due to the fact that they were not Chinese. They were denounced

[1] San Francisco newspapers.

as foreigners, but while they held the high offices in Peking and the provinces, the towns and villages carried on local government according to ancient custom. It is estimated that the Manchus numbered about 5,000,000 out of a population of 400,000,000. The people felt the hand of the Manchu government through its viceroys in the provinces, where they were often guilty of extortion and other arbitrary measures.

The revolution which Sun Yat Sen planned was different from previous uprisings, which had as their object a change of rulers. Dr. Sun advocated a change of the system of government.

It is difficult to understand how Sun Yat Sen imagined that the Chinese were ready for any sort of republic. The obstacles were stupendous. About nine out of ten of the people were illiterate; there was no common spoken language; and the written characters were complicated and difficult even for scholars. Means of internal communication existed only where there were rivers or canals; most of the people were always on the verge of starvation and were only interested in getting enough to eat. Yet Sun was striving to establish a form of government which demands a literate population interested in public affairs.

Another hindrance was the absence of a national consciousness. There was racial and cultural consciousness, and the task before Sun and his followers was to arouse a sense of nationality. This the younger people began to feel.

Dr. Sun never seemed to recognize the tremendous difficulties in his way until shortly before his death, and even then he did not materially change his views. So most foreigners and many thoughtful Chinese considered him an impractical theorist, a persistent trouble-maker, and a blatant demagogue. In spite of all hin-drances, however, he went about the world making converts and raising money to carry on his propaganda.

## CHAPTER VIII

# The Attempted Revolt of 1900

## Conditions in China and a Second Conspiracy That Failed

AFTER the suppression of the reform movement of 1898, the old Dowager Empress again ruled China. The humiliating defeat of China by the Japanese in the war of 1894–95 should have taught her that the strength of Japan was due to her adoption of modern scientific methods, but it did not.

This extraordinary woman had originally been a concubine of the Emperor Hsien Feng. She managed by unscrupulous scheming to gain power. When she bore a son, as mother of the heir-apparent she obtained the strong position which Chinese custom gave her, and when the Emperor died she became the ruler of China. She had all the prejudices of the old order with its contempt for foreigners and foreign learning and customs. On the death of the Emperor she got rid of all the nobles who stood in her way and ruled with a rod of iron.

Her son died young, leaving an unborn child, so that she continued her regency. She was always ready to pounce upon anyone who seemed to be dangerous to her power. That was the reason she made a prisoner of the Emperor and declared the reform edicts null and void. She knew through her spies of the movement in

Kwangtung, of which Sun Yat Sen was the leader, and was ready to go to any length to put it down.

Then came the Boxer movement in 1900 and the outbreak in which so many foreigners were killed when those devoted to the old order were determined to drive them from the country. The Boxers were really carrying out the policy of her hatred of these "barbarians." At the back of all the trouble was the hatred of aliens and their aggressive policy, accompanied by the fear that the ancient customs of China were in danger through their teaching and influence. The slogan of the Boxers was: "Protect the country, destroy the foreigners."

One would have thought that the old Empress would have known by this time something of the power of the despised foreign nations, but she was profoundly ignorant of the outside world. She gave the Boxers encouragement, for they were carrying into effect her view of the self-sufficiency of China.

The disturbances were in the north and there the allies landed for the march to Peking, where the Legations and others were besieged in their place of refuge. The American, British, French, German, Japanese, and Russian troops easily dispersed the Chinese army and took Peking. The Empress and her court fled to the west and the allies looted the city, the conduct of some of them being like that of savage Huns rather than soldiers of nominally Christian nations.

During most of the period of the Boxer trouble, Sun Yat Sen was abroad seeking funds. The disturbances in the north only strengthened him in his purpose to effect a revolution. He knew foreign nations and what discipline and modern arms can do with a disorganized mob.

He saw more plainly than ever before that to finance a modern revolt required a large sum of money for preparation and the purchase of arms and ammunition. This money he set out to obtain in the United States and Europe. The amount he wanted was $2,500,000, more than he could hope to get from contributions. In an interview concerning this he said: "I began to canvass for political funds. I traveled in America and visited the leading bankers in Europe. Emissaries sent by me penetrated into all quarters. Some professing to act in my name proved faithless, but I prefer not to speak of them."

He does not say whether he succeeded in getting any advances based on the chance of his future success, but what he was told later by a Frenchman no doubt held good then. This was that the French were not likely to lend money unless they had ample security, which Sun certainly was not able to give. He did, however, get large sums in the aggregate from subscriptions made in all parts of the world; and with this money he carried on his work of propaganda and, as far as he had means, made arrangements for a supply of arms and ammunition.

One method he used to obtain funds was to issue paper money. The notes were for ten dollars and were issued by "The Chang Hwa Republic," under which title was a blue flag with a white sun in the center. They promised to pay the bearer ten dollars in gold on the formation of the Republic, at its treasury or by its agents abroad. They were signed, Sun Wen, President, and Gnone Hap, Treasurer. These notes were exchanged for coin by Sun and his agents in all parts of

the world where there were Chinese, and in this way
a goodly sum of money found its way into the treasury.
The notes were printed in Chinese and English.

With all the difficulties which confronted him, a less
determined man would have given up long ago, but
hardship seemed only to spur him on to greater efforts.
In order to have headquarters in a safe place as near to
China as possible, he established a base in Yokohama
where there were many Chinese. At the foot of the
Bluff where the Europeans and Americans lived, not far
from the Grand Hotel, so well known to all travelers,
there was a house where the members of the revolutionary society could come and go. From this house, which
was not far from the Chinese Consulate, correspondence was kept up with the groups of Young China in
Canton and wherever the society had members.

Preparations were made for an uprising in the latter
part of 1900. A contingent of the progressive party had
been drilled, led by officers trained under foreign supervision, for there were sympathizers with Sun Yat Sen,
both Caucasian and Japanese. But the force was small
and it was an audacious thing to imagine that the young
men composing it could overcome the armies of the
powerful Manchus. The expectation was, as in the
revolt of 1895, that after the initial success multitudes
would flock to their standard. Where they expected to
get arms and ammunition for a large force is a question,
and on later occasions failure was said to be due to lack
of ammunition.

When all was supposed to be ready, Sun Yat Sen left
Yokohama for Hongkong; but on his arrival at that
port the British authorities, who had been informed by
the Peking government of the intended uprising, would

not allow him to land. The revolutionists had gathered in a valley, not far from Macao, the entrances to which were carefully guarded, where they were to await the leader. The treasurer of the society, who had come by an earlier steamer, had likewise not been permitted to land and had been taken to Singapore. There Sun also went. The treasurer had a large sum of money which was required for the enterprise; and the leader, when he reached Singapore, found that the treasurer had been arrested and the money taken from him. It took considerable time for Dr. Sun to put in the claim that the money belonged to him and that he needed it for purposes of trade, but after vexatious delay he got the authorities to return it to him.

With all possible haste Sun Yat Sen reached Hongkong and this time he was allowed to land. But he was so closely watched by the British officials that he could not get to the place where his followers were assembled. All he could do was to send a message telling them to go across the country to a certain position and he would manage somehow to meet them there. But by this time the opportunity had passed, owing to the delay, and the revolutionists were attacked by the Imperial troops. Though they reached the appointed place, they realized that their plans had again failed, and the men were scattered to their homes. The time which had been lost while Sun was at Singapore made a surprise impossible; there had been time for the spies to inform the officials at Canton that armed men were gathering not far from the city, and at once soldiers were sent against them.

This wild adventure occurred in September, 1900. The revolutionists numbered only about six hundred.

The intention had been to capture the small town of Waichow, when an uprising was expected elsewhere. It was then hoped that the province of Fukien could be subjugated, and this done the Republic of China was to be declared. But all plans were upset when some four thousand Imperial troops caused the small force under Sun to flee for safety.

In this outbreak, Sun had expected assistance from the Bow Wongs, but this failed to materialize. The Bow Wong Society was an organization which advocated constitutional reform, but its members were not in sympathy with the revolutionary tactics of Sun and it is difficult to see how he expected aid from them.

From every point of view the cause of the revolutionists seemed hopeless after this fiasco, and no doubt it would have been thought so, had it not been for the irrepressible Sun. Despite this last failure he set to work with renewed energy for another attempt, both by propaganda and preparation.

In this uprising Chinese students from Tokyo had taken an active part. Not all of these were with the little band of rebels in the field; many of the young men from Japan had returned to their homes in various parts of China, and wherever they went they disseminated revolutionary doctrine. In a number of places they had organized secret societies which, later on, proved most helpful to the revolutionary party. Their residence in Japan had convinced them that if an oriental nation was to awaken from the sleep of satisfaction with itself, it must have education in the modern way and adopt scientific methods in industry and warfare. One of these students, named Tong Choy, had organized a society in Hankow and had attempted an uprising in that city, at the same time that Sun had gathered his small force near Canton. It was easily put down, and those who took part in it and had the misfortune to be captured were executed in the usual way.

Testimony as to the influence exercised in China by men who had been under foreign training was given by Mrs. Francis Hawkes Pott, a Chinese woman, the wife of an American who was the president of St. John's College, Shanghai. Some forty boys had gone at different times from Honolulu to study at St. John's, and on one occasion she addressed their parents and friends. She said that the boys who had come from Honolulu had changed the spirit of the institution. When asked to explain what she meant, she said:

The students you have sent us did their preparatory work in your public and private schools. In these they grew up in daily contact and intimate association with American boys, who were intensely patriotic. When they came to Shanghai they found our students possessed a pride of race, but they lacked national consciousness and had no patriotic sentiment. Somehow your boys aroused in them a love of their country and a desire to see it take its place among the great nations of the world.

The Hawaiian contingent, which was quite large, saw for the first time China as it was, and when they compared the condition of the people with that in the land in which they were born, they were fired with a desire to have a part in aiding the land of their fathers to cast off the wrappings which bound it to the unchanging past.

Perhaps the greatest change they brought about was in respect to sports. All your boys had been members of football or baseball teams, and they brought with them the spirit and the practice of sport. They taught our students that it was not beneath the dignity of a scholar to engage in healthful outdoor games. This was a very great gain for in sports our young men learned the benefit of team work and the love of fair play.

In saying that returned students kindled a spirit of patriotism among the youth of China, it must not be implied that all of them became revolutionists, although many of them did; but it does mean that all saw the need of reform. Many of the graduates of St. John's, who had spent their boyhood in Hawaii, later occupied high places in the Peking or reform governments. Among these have been foreign secretaries, ambassadors, consuls, and one prime minister; many held prominent places in various departments of the state, or gained high positions in law or medicine. A number of these had done preparatory work at Iolani School, the one Sun Yat Sen attended for about six years in Honolulu. What is said of St. John's may be said of other institutions. Their graduates, having been under the influence of foreign teachers, as well as those who had been abroad, carried enlightenment to all parts of China. This must be understood in order to account for the "student movement" which assumed such importance later. These students were zealous for the education of the people and for modern methods of government, and imbued with a hatred of the corruption that permeated all official life under the old system. Young China, in many communities throughout the country, prepared the way for the final revolution in 1911, when the Manchu dynasty was overthrown.

## CHAPTER IX

# Abroad Again

Sun Goes to Honolulu in 1903. Then to San

Francisco, New York, London, and

Back to China

AFTER the failure of 1900 Sun Yat Sen spent some time in Japan with headquarters in Yokohama. He kept in close touch with the local organizations by correspondence, and laid plans for the next uprising. In 1903 he determined to make a journey round the world to stir up enthusiasm and to collect funds.

He arrived in Honolulu on October 5, on the steamer *Siberia,* and at once went to the house of friends. For some time he kept quiet, meeting his sympathizers in private houses and inspiring them with hope for the future. On December 13 he held his first public meeting in the Hotel Street Theater which was filled with his countrymen. At this time most of the Chinese in Hawaii still wore the cue and Chinese clothes, and the fact that Sun was unlike them led a reporter to write that "he had on a linen suit, his hair was cropped short, so that he looked like a Filipino."

By constant practice he had become an orator of considerable power and he emphasized his words with impressive gestures. The report of the meeting stated that he did not give the impression of being a fanatic. He evidently moved the hearts of the audience for he was frequently applauded. What he said on this occasion was nothing new, but he maintained that nothing but a revolution would lift China out of its deplorable condition. Other dynasties had been overthrown, and if the people would rise the Manchus could be driven out. He had every reason to believe that all would soon be ready for the final blow. The country was weak because the government was corrupt and incompetent, so that in the Boxer trouble twenty thousand foreign soldiers took Peking. There were millions of men in China who would make good soldiers if there were leaders able to give them modern training, whom they could trust. The revolution would be successful in time. The people must be aroused and the help of all was needed to accomplish this.

On December 21, he gave to the Honolulu English press the substance of his message to his countrymen:

We must develop a spirit of nationalism among the Chinese who are not Manchus; this is my life work. Once this spirit is awakened the Chinese nation will rise in the might of its four hundred million people and overthrow the Manchu dynasty forever. Then the republic will be erected, for the great provinces of China are like the States of the American Union, and what we need is a President to govern all alike.[1]

He then went on to trace the history of the Manchus and to tell of their offenses. He contrasted the patriotism of the Japanese with the clan spirit of China; there was no patriotism in China because there was no country they could call their own. The Chinese Government had sent a thousand students to Japan, but the Manchus among these had informed the Imperial Government of the actions of the Chinese of pure blood and had asked

[1] This passage and the information in following paragraphs were taken from the *Honolulu Advertiser,* December 14 and 21, 1903.

that these should not be permitted to enter the universities or military schools. The Chinese Minister to Japan had endeavored to stop meetings of the students to discuss the subject of Chinese nationality.

With this action on the part of the Imperial Government, Sun could hardly find fault, for it was well known that these students in Japan—although they were being educated at the expense of that Government —were not loyal to it and were secretly plotting to overthrow it. He concluded his message in these words:

We are men without a country. When we go to foreign lands and we are assaulted, the Imperial Government does not care for us. Why do you wear the cue? It is a sign of Manchu supremacy. To disobey this order, in China, would mean decapitation for you.

Many of us fear that the Powers will divide China. If we do not assist them they cannot do it. Some say that we ought to have a constitutional monarchy, but that is out of the question. There is no reason why we cannot have a republic. China is already a rudimentary republic.

This last is evidently addressed to the Bow Wongs, who advocated a constitutional monarchy; there were many of these in Honolulu, where they had organized a society to promote their idea. It was associated with those of like views in China, but the Manchus had as yet given no hint that they would consider any reform in that line, although they did shortly after this, when they feared the revolutionists.

Sun Yat Sen remained in Hawaii for six months, spending a part of the time at Kula, Island of Maui, where his mother and his wife and children lived with his elder brother, Ah Mi, who was now quite reconciled to the younger man and in sympathy with his revolutionary endeavors. While he was there, on March 9, 1904, he obtained the certificate stating that he was born in the Islands, as has been related, and was consequently an American citizen.

On March 31, he sailed for San Francisco on the *Korea*, intending to visit cities in the United States on his way eastward by way of Suez to China where the next revolt was shortly to be staged. Before he left he was more outspoken than usual; he openly said that he expected to be in China before autumn and then the great movement for the overturning of the Manchus would begin. He was full of hope that this time he would be successful, for the people were awakening and the plans were perfected. When someone said to him, "Some day I hope to hear of you as the president of the Chinese Republic," he smiled and shrugged his shoulders.

Armed with his birth certificate he thought there would be no difficulty in landing in San Francisco, but he was mistaken. The United States officials had been advised that he was coming and also that Prince Po Lun was to arrive from China on his way to the St. Louis Exposition. It was thought that this archrevolutionist might do the Manchu Prince some harm, perhaps might try to assassinate him, so something was found to be wrong with Dr. Sun's papers and he was placed in the quarters provided for the detention of immigrants until inquiry was made. He was kept there until the Prince had landed and was not liberated for over a week after Po Lun had left the city. Sun Yat Sen had never advocated assassination and had never attempted to get rid of his enemies by that method.

On being given his liberty, he went to Chinatown and

took up his quarters in the Chinese Society of English
Education. He at once began to work among his countrymen; and his activities did not escape the attention of
the Chinese Consul General, who issued a warning
which was published in the papers:

There is a revolutionary leader in our midst, who is arousing people by his false statements. The educated element can
easily understand that his aim is to collect money which he will
afterwards squander, and I fear the ignorant people will become his victims. As the chief—the Consul General—here, it
is my duty to protect them. I advise the elder people who will
not be turned by his false utterances, to control their younger
brothers and sons to beware of this man. He will squander
your money and get you into trouble. [Signed] Consul General Chung.[1]

This, however, did not prevent Dr. Sun from speaking
in public; he made an address in the Washington Street
Theater before a large audience. On this occasion he is
reported to have said that he had never been in San
Francisco before; but there would have been no object
in saying this, and besides many of the Chinese remembered well that he had been there in 1896 and had collected money for revolutionary purposes.

He was carefully watched while he stayed in San
Francisco, and there was a rumor that the Consul General had communicated with the Department of State
requesting that a bodyguard of secret service men be
designated to guard Prince Po Lun against a possible
attack at St. Louis. This may have been done, for Sun
Yat Sen went to St. Louis where he made a short stay,
and then went on to New York. There he had friends
whom he had known in China; one of them was Tong
Phong who had been baptized at the same time with

[1] *San Francisco Examiner,* May, 1904.

Sun in Hongkong. The time was drawing near for the
next uprising and he soon sailed for London. There he
embarked for the Orient by way of the Suez Canal; he
made a short stop at Singapore and reached China without mishap.

By this time Sun Yat Sen believed that the organization of the revolutionists was perfected. He was its un-
disputed head, and the branches of the society, which
met of course in secret, had each its elected leader. In
the provinces north of Kwangtung, the larger cities had
their local organizations, about forty in all, each said to
have a thousand members, ready to rise at a moment's
notice. Men had been selected to take charge of public
affairs in the districts where the organizations existed.

Every precaution had been taken, the places where
meetings were held were frequently changed. No letters
were written and communication was kept up by means
of messengers. It was fully believed that the soldiers
were ready to join the revolutionists. Systematic instruction had been given in regard to obedience to orders
and to living up to the rules and regulations of the
society. It was feared that when the uprising occurred
the people would become disorganized, and the plan
was to keep the mob under control. Every precaution
possible was taken to prevent disloyalty, for Sun was
afraid that dread of torture might lead some weak
members of the society to become traitors and reveal
its plans to the officials.

It had taken years of patient work to bring all this
about, but everything was now ready. When foreigners
spoke of Sun Yat Sen as an "unstable idealist" and as
a "vagabond conspirator," they did not give him credit
for the organizing ability showed by his plan, of which

they were ignorant. It was this systematic organization which at last brought about success. One or two Europeans who had interviews with him were impressed then, and later, by his personality, his evident sincerity, and the power he had over men. He was not a mere itinerant trouble-maker, but the leader of a movement which was spreading over the whole of China. He was reserved, as most Chinese are; he was suspicious, a racial characteristic which was especially observable in him; he was deceptive, as his experiences had forced him to be; but without elements of greatness he could not have obtained and held the leadership of a movement which was to convulse China, to overturn an empire, and to involve the chief Powers of the world.

## CHAPTER X

# The Unlucky Plan of Revolt in 1904

## Sun's Narrow Escape from Capture

AFTER years of preparation the time was judged ripe for another attempt to overthrow the Manchu dynasty and establish the Republic of China. The revolutionists had obtained a good supply of arms and ammunition; the secret organizations in south China and elsewhere had been notified to be ready; and distant groups had also received word that the time was at hand.

The Chinese Consul at Honolulu had sent word to the Viceroy at Canton that the Progressives in Hawaii were active in the movement, giving, as far as he could, the names and residences in China of the families of those who were enrolled as conspirators in the Islands. The Honolulu Chinese knew of this, and being only too aware of the custom of holding the relatives of rebels responsible for the action of their children and brothers, they naturally felt alarm. But in some way news came to Hawaii of information to the Consul that too many people in Kwangtung Province would be affected if any retaliatory steps were taken, and nothing could be done. Besides this, the parents and relations of the Progressives were in ignorance of the course taken by the deluded young men in Honolulu.

Among the attendants at meetings held in Honolulu by Sun Yat Sen was a youth who, while in his teens, had been sworn in to the Hung Chung Hui, the Progressive Society. His name was Chang Chau. He had been born in Hawaii and was an ardent supporter of the movement for the enlightenment of the land of his fathers. When he took the oath as a junior member of the society, Dr. Sun, who had taken a liking to the young man, said, "I receive you as a sworn brother, you must come when I call you." Chang was a Hakka; but like the Honolulu Chinese generally, he understood Punti, the dialect in which the meetings were conducted.

In 1904 he received a call to go to China, and at once left for the headquarters at Yokohama. There he learned something of the plans which had been made, and received instructions as to where he would meet Sun Yat Sen. He sailed for Hongkong accompanied by some of the Chinese students who had also received the call for active service. At Hongkong he found great activity at headquarters and learned from the leaders much of what was expected to take place. They believed that the yamen, with its arsenal containing arms and ammunition, could be taken without difficulty, and many of the soldiers were known to be ready to join them. The various groups were waiting to be notified, and when these had gathered they could declare the Republic and march northward. There organized societies were only waiting for an initial success to conduct local uprisings. Everything looked favorable and all were hopeful and enthusiastic.

The steamer which leaves Hongkong at midnight reaches Canton by daylight and Chang Chau and those with him were soon lost in the great city with its teeming multitudes. They made their way to the headquarters, which were situated near the place where the Church of Our Saviour, a mission of the Church of England, now stands. There are many secret societies in Canton, so that gatherings of men do not necessarily arouse suspicion; and to avoid observation, the policy of the revolutionists had been to have small groups meet at various places. Only the leaders met at the headquarters, to which Chang Chau was directed; there he found Sun Yat Sen. As the sworn brother of the leader, Chang was to be near him as his trusted aide. In fact, many times during this revolt and the next one, these two men occupied the same bed and always slept in the same room. Sun had stayed for weeks at a time at the home of the Honolulu man; and as far as any one was allowed to be, the young follower was in the secrets of the older leader, both as to his present plans and as to events in his past life. So his information is valuable, especially when checked with other trust-worthy accounts.

Arrangements had been made for a shipment of ten barrels of pistols and ammunition from Hongkong, con-signed to a merchant as Portland cement, and this was expected soon to supplement supplies on hand at vari-ous places. A steamer had been chartered to bring three thousand armed men from Hongkong, and to these had been assigned the duty of keeping order and controlling the populace while Sun Yat Sen and his picked men, coming from their several quarters, gathered at a cer-tain point near the yamen, which they expected to take easily. If resistance was offered, these men were to do the fighting.

In addition to the three thousand men, another steamer was to bring seven hundred coolies as steerage passengers. These were to do the needful carrying and fetching, after the yamen was captured. They were not in the secret but had been told someone would meet them on arrival and take them to their work. Travelers who have seen the crowd of coolies on a steamer plying between Hongkong and Canton, packed in the steerage, lying on the floor of the lower deck close together, can understand that a few hundred of them would excite no comment or suspicion.

All was ready. The leaders were at the Society's headquarters; runners had been sent out to the various local groups; all incriminating papers had been burned; and units, each with its allotted work, were ready to start. Everything had gone well so far; there had been no hitch and no suspicion had been aroused in the minds of the officials. Just then a telegram was received from Hongkong saying that something had happened and that the three thousand men could not come. Whether the British officials had got news of the expedition and had delayed the steamer for investigation was never fully known. All plans were upset. A wire was sent in all haste to Hongkong to stop the coolies, but unfortunately the message was misunderstood. When the coolies arrived, there was no one to meet them and they wandered about the city.

Misfortunes seemed to pile up. The barrels of pistols arrived; and as they were being unloaded from the vessel, one barrel fell out of its sling, broke as it struck the landing, and exposed its contents. News was at once taken to the Viceroy that something suspicious was going on.

The Viceroy did not believe this was evidence that any uprising was at hand, for his spies had no information as to any plot. But when word came that several hundred coolies had come from Hongkong and had expected someone to meet them, orders were given to hunt them down. A number of them were caught, imprisoned, and in a short time executed. The poor fellows were entirely ignorant of any contemplated revolt; but since they could give no account of themselves, even under torture, they were beheaded as an example to those who might be conspirators.

At the headquarters, as soon as it was known that the Viceroy had been informed of the accident to the barrel of pistols, there was consternation. Sun ordered the men to scatter. However, the leaders were diligently sought; and sixteen persons, who had been seen around the headquarters, were arrested and later beheaded. Many of these were entirely innocent; but such a thing as a trial was unknown, the life of a man being nothing to the Viceroy. The only way to make sure that no guilty man should escape was to cut off the head of every man taken.

Sun Yat Sen and his sworn brother, Chang Chau, reached the Bund, or quay, by devious alleys, such as abound in Canton; there hundreds of boats were to be found, many of them in charge of women. Into one of these the two men entered. Making some excuse of hiding from pursuers, Sun, who always carried a quantity of gold in a belt, offered the women a goodly sum if they would furnish him and his companion with women's clothes and take them over the river to a place which they named. The money offered was enough to tempt any poor Chinese boatwoman; the boat was pulled out from the quay, the men went into the covered part of it and were soon attired in the working clothes of the women who live on the river.

On the way eastward from the Bund in Canton, Shameen, the foreign concession, lies to the right, separated from the Chinese city by a narrow stream crossed by a bridge. To the left of Shameen, at some little distance, is a large church of the Berlin Mission, and to this the boatwomen were directed. This church was the center of a group of some five hundred men who were waiting for the word to march to Canton. The minister, a Chinese, was the leader of the revolutionists at this point, and nearly all of the men under him were Christians, members of his congregation. Sun and Chang made their way to the church, which was not far from the landing, and told the men who had gathered there that the game was up, that a series of misfortunes had upset all their well-laid plans, and that they must scatter, each man looking out for his own safety.

This done, Sun and Chang, still dressed as boatwomen, went to the landing and found there a side-wheeled steamer owned by Chinese. Going into the steerage, they took their places with the rest of the passengers bound for Hongkong. Women of the class they represented wear a kind of bonnet made of dark blue cotton cloth, the color of their clothes, which covers the head somewhat like an abbreviated sunbonnet. As neither Sun nor Chang had cues, the disguise was complete. They carried false cues, for use when it suited their purpose, which could easily be arranged under a close-fitting Chinese hat, something like a skullcap.

In Hongkong, Sun had plenty of friends and the two remained secluded for a few days until they sailed— Dr. Sun for Singapore and Chang Chau for Honolulu.

For the third time Sun Yat Sen had failed in his attempts at revolt. This last time the preparation had been more thorough than on other occasions. The first was an audacious venture in which probably not more than five hundred men had actually been engaged. The second was planned on a larger scale, but if Sun had been allowed to land at Hongkong it scarcely could have succeeded unless great numbers had flocked to his standard after the expected initial success. The third attempt seemed to have been well prepared, but the series of misfortunes upset all the plans. Again the revolutionists were scattered and in hiding.

Some of Sun's most intimate associates advised him to give up further efforts, but he would not hear of it. He was determined to go on until he prevailed, however long it took. Like Bruce of Scotland, even though he failed seven times he would go on trying, for he believed that the people were increasingly favorable to the cause to which he had dedicated his life.

## CHAPTER XI

# New Preparations for Revolution

## The Outbreak of 1907. Sun Escapes Disguised as a Beggar

IN 1904, after Sun's escape from Canton, he spent two days in Hongkong and then sailed for Singapore and the Straits Settlements, where he had many friends and supporters. Hongkong was too near Canton and with the huge price of $750,000, Mexican, on his head, it was dangerous to remain there. In Singapore he would be in comparative safety; and the Chinese there, numbering upward of a million, were generally favorable to his cause. It is a wonder that, with the great reward offered, some of his followers did not betray him, but there is no intimation anywhere that an attempt of this kind was made. There were men whom he trusted to collect money who failed him—one agent collected $2,000 and decamped for parts unknown—but none of his adherents tried to deliver him to his enemies. Those in the society never lost faith in the unselfishness and integrity of the leader who went about the world keeping alive the spirit of hope for the future.

During the years from 1904 to 1907, he spent his time in preaching the revolutionary doctrine and encouraging the local societies. To all those who believed in constitutional reform under the Manchus, he said that the only hope for China was their overthrow and the establishment of a republic. He knew of the failure of the attempt at reform in 1898 and what happened to the young Emperor and those who tried to promote it.

The old Dowager Empress kept herself well informed and the sporadic uprisings and the report of the attempted revolution of Sun Yat Sen in 1904 in Canton alarmed her. But what led her and her advisers to see that changes must be made, if the dynasty was to be saved, was the result of the war between Russia and Japan in 1904–5. It was evident that the reason Japan was victorious was that she had adopted modern methods.

The Dowager Empress saw that something must be done and the first step was taken in 1905, when picked men were sent to foreign countries to study their systems of government and all other matters which were important to China. On the report of these investigators, in 1906, a constitution was promised; the laws were to be revised; finances were to be reorganized; the army and navy were to be placed on a modern footing; a police force was to be established; and western education was to be inaugurated at several centers. In order to get the people interested in the affairs of government, both local and Imperial, efforts were to be made by publication to disseminate information.

On its face all this looked very favorable. If the proposed reforms had been carried out, much of the program for which the Progressives stood would have been achieved.

Sun Yat Sen and his followers did not believe, however, that the Empress was sincere; and in any event the chief grievance in their minds, the rule of the Manchus, would still be in force. As long as they were in power there would be a despotism, and Dr. Sun was a republican by principle.

So the Progressives did not cease to agitate and to prepare, nor did the promised reforms put a stop to outbreaks. Perhaps disorders were useful in convincing Peking that discontent was still in existence, but the movements which occurred seemed to be ill timed and futile. In 1906, outbreaks took place at Ping-heon and at Lai-lin; in both cases, there was some fighting, but the insurgents were poorly supplied with ammunition and those who did not escape suffered for their temerity.

In 1907 Sun Yat Sen believed that his preparations were again perfected and determined to start in a new direction. Three times Canton had been the center of revolt; the immediate object had been the seizure of the yamen, the headquarters of the government, with its stores of arms and ammunition. All these attempts had resulted in miserable failures. This time the plan was to commence activity in the district to the north of the French territory of Tonkin.

While this was being contemplated, there were several local outbreaks. In the early part of 1907, a fight occurred at Hupeh where a force under Gen. Wang Hing took the field and had to flee. In May a Manchu official of high rank started trouble for some reason, with the usual result. In July there was a movement in Swatow. While all these were unimportant, they served to show the widespread dissatisfaction with the existing order. At this time, in July, 1907, word was being sent out to the local branches of the Progressives designating the place where men were to congregate. It had been agreed that those who had pledged themselves to support the cause by their presence should at once set out for China on receipt of the word "Come." On August 15, Chang Chau, in Honolulu, received a cablegram containing the one word which was to him a command. What he did is related because it illustrates what happened in many places—San Francisco, Singapore, Japan, wherever organizations of revolutionists existed.

Chang Chau had just commenced work with a large firm, but he at once notified the manager that he had received word calling him at once to China on important business. He hastily notified those who were to go with him and left that same night on a steamer which happened to be in the harbor. As the sworn brother of Sun, he did not hesitate, and he knew that he would be useful because he was familiar with western customs and spoke English well.

When he reached Yokohama he received instructions at the headquarters of the Progressive Society. He was to take charge of twenty young men who had been students; they had specialized in chemistry, and were able to make dynamite and manufacture bombs. He arranged for their passage to Hongkong where they were to receive a message as to their destination. Upon their arrival in that city they were told to take a certain steamer to Haiphong on the Gulf of Tonkin. On their way the steamer called at Pakhoi, a port at the head of the gulf, which is in the Chinese province of Kwangsi.

What followed shows the danger to which the men who were congregating from all directions were exposed. The steamer was Chinese, and the officials came on board to inspect the ship and the passengers, these last being lined up on deck as is customary with oriental steerage passengers. Chang had the idea that information had been sent to the officials to be on the outlook for him and his party, and as a consequence he was almost paralyzed with fear. This belief seemed to be a certainty, when he saw that the inspection was being made by a naval officer. He fully expected that he and his men would be arrested, and he had visions of the torture chamber, and an awful death.

The followers of Dr. Sun had a secret sign by which they could recognize each other; and as the Admiral—for so the officer proved to be—came down the line, the terrified Chang involuntarily placed his right hand over his heart, which seemed to him to be about to stop beating. When he did this, the Admiral, who was abreast of him, looked into his eyes and then placed his hand in the position of the countersign which would announce that he too was a revolutionist. Chang, without intending to do so, had given the sign of the society, and when he saw the reply he at first thought it must be a trick to catch him. He could not believe that the officer was one of the plotters, but when he passed on without a word and nothing was done the relief was intense. His mouth was so dry from fear that he could not speak, and he and his men looked at each other scarcely believing that nothing was to happen to them.

When the steamer reached Haiphong the party went up the Song Koi River to Hanoi, the capital of Tonkin, where they met Sun Yat Sen. Chang told him of the fright on the steamer and of the officer giving the countersign, and Sun drew a paper from his pocket which showed that the Admiral was one of them and only waiting for success on land to join the revolution openly. That this was not an improbable case was shown by the action of the navy later in 1911. At the time, in 1907, Dr. Sun knew that there were land and naval

forces ready to cast in their lot with him as soon as he
had gained some striking initial advantage. This union
of trained men with his undisciplined crowd had been
hoped for on each occasion of an uprising, but Sun
never seemed to recognize the meagerness of the re-
sources of his party and the difficulty of overcoming a
body of troops with any sort of training. The army and
navy had many officers and men in sympathy with the
aims of the Progressives, but they were not going to
risk their lives until there was some chance of victory.

In October the campaign opened in the province of
Yunnan, which lies to the north of Tonkin. Several
small towns were taken; but when the rebels met the
Imperial troops they found that their supply of ammunition had given out, so that they had to retire in dis-
orderly flight into French territory.

It was each man for himself, and among the fugitives were Sun Yat Sen and Chang Chau. They had
been together as close companions since they met at
Hanoi, and for the second time they were seeking safety
together. They had a narrow escape from capture after
the fighting, but they managed to get to a village at the
entrance of which they came across two beggars. Sun
at once accosted them and proposed an exchange of
clothes, offering them $20 in gold. To the beggars this
sum of money would be great riches; amounting, as it
then did, to about $46, Mexican, it would keep them in
comfort many months. The four went into a hovel;
Sun and Chang were soon clad in the disreputable garments of the beggars, and when the fugitives rubbed
dirt on their faces their disguise was perfect. They made
their way to the river, Song Koi, and there took passage in a junk for Hongkong.

Sun was again urged to give up further attempts at revolution, but he once more declared that he would go on until the people of China rose and overthrew their oppressors.

## CHAPTER XII

# The First Triumph

Sun in Japan and America, Preparing for 1911.
The News of a Premature Outbreak. He
Goes to England Hoping To Secure a
Loan. His Election as President
of China

THE old Dowager Empress died in 1908; and the next year the Assembly, which she had promised should be called, was chosen by a restricted electorate. To satisfy the revolutionists, or to pacify them, a sort of fictitious parliament met, with a senate nominated by the regent. It was, as Sun had expected, largely a farce.

The people of China were being educated as to abuses and the need of reform by newspapers and magazines, the increase in the number of which was astonishing. The first Chinese newspaper was published in Shanghai in 1870. A revolutionary paper, called *China*, was started in Hongkong in 1900. By 1910 there were, it is estimated, five hundred papers and magazines published in China. With nine out of ten people illiterate— some authorities say more—one might ask how these publications could reach the masses. The answer is that in the halls of the guilds, the secret societies, the village tea houses, and in homes, the people gathered and those who were literate read to eager listeners the news and articles relating to reform.

The plan of widespread education promised by the dynasty was in a chaotic state, but the foreign schools and colleges continued their work of giving the students a modern education. The foreign middle schools, some of which were called colleges, numbered fifty-seven, twenty-five of these being American and a like number British, nearly all of which had been founded and were maintained by the Protestant missions. The Roman Catholics had established five. There were two general colleges, one of which was the Hongkong University. Besides these, there were medical schools connected with the hospitals in various parts of the country. Further, there were the many students who had been educated in the United States of America and in Europe. The veneration for learning, which the Chinese have, gave the students trained in these institutions an influence beyond calculation, especially when, combined with modern learning, the young men and women had a good knowledge of Chinese. For many years practically all education on western lines in China was the result of the work of the mission institutions, carried on despite opposition and misrepresentation.

When Sun Yat Sen told the American people, "Our greatest hope is to make the Bible and Christian education, as we have come to know them in America and Europe, the basis of reform in China,"[1] he must have meant that the people needed not only a knowledge of modern science and political methods, but a new conception of life and an aroused conscience as to their

---

[1] Words spoken at a public meeting in San Francisco, according to a newspaper report.

relations to God and man. Yet, at times, he seemed to think that the ballot and representative government, under a constitution, would remedy all the evils existing in his country. He was not different from those in the United States and elsewhere who believed that the ballot box and secular education would eliminate crime, and that the best men would always be elected if all men had the vote. He was hopeful and went bravely on with the work of propaganda, biding his time and directing his followers, from Japan or from any place where he might be. It is unnecessary, if not impossible, to follow his course as he went from country to country. In the years between 1907 and 1911 he visited Singapore, Tonkin, Hongkong, Japan, Hawaii, the mainland of the United States, England, and France, and then went back by way of the Suez Canal to China.

During these years of preparation Sun Yat Sen was frequently in Japan, where he sometimes remained for months. He could readily pass for a Japanese, as has been shown, although he could not speak the language, except a few common words. In 1906 there was a quite large population of Chinese in Yokohama, where the headquarters of the Progressives were, and among these he worked, keeping in constant communication with the organizations in China.

At that time the Rev. Teiichi Hori, later in charge of a church in Honolulu, was pastor of a Japanese Congregational Church in Yokohama. He was brought in contact with Sun and others of the revolutionary party and his story is of interest. He says:

After Sun Yat Sen left in 1906, the agent of the American Bible Society brought to my house and introduced to me Mr. Chun, the secretary of Dr. Sun, who had been directed to stay in Yokohama and carry on the work of the Progressive Society. Soon after this, I found a letter on my desk in Chinese characters, with which I am familiar, telling me that he was in trouble and needed a friend and asking me to come and see him. I went to his lodgings and found that the Chinese Consul had received information that he was in the city, and had brought it to the attention of the Japanese authorities stating that Chun was fomenting a revolution and interesting Japanese as well as Chinese. The result was that Chun had been notified that he must leave Japan and that he could go to any country he pleased.

Chun knew that I was in sympathy with Sun Yat Sen and his ideals and asked my advice and assistance, as he wanted to stay in Japan where he had important duties to perform. We talked the matter over and I decided to take him to my house, which I did under cover of darkness. We felt that the best way was to dress him as a Japanese, so my wife set to work to make him Japanese clothes, including a kimono, which, at that time was more generally worn by our countrymen in cities than it is now. When he was fitted out I thought it best for him not to remain in my house longer, so I took him to a boarding house near by, whose proprietor was known to me. I told him I had brought a friend whom I wished to have stay with him. I said that he had gone abroad when a very small child and he had forgotten his Japanese. He stayed there about four months, until Sun came back from America and remained six months in the country. Sun was frequently at my house and we became good friends. He trusted me and was grateful to me and we had long talks about his affairs. He was very hopeful and said he was sure of success in the end, by the help of God. Those were the very words he used, for he had told me he was a Christian. I do not think he went to church in Yokohama for he could not have understood what was said.

He moved to Tokyo where he became friends with many of the professors of Waseda University, and during his stay there he met Count Okuma, who, of course, could not express sympathy but was interested in him. The Japanese Christians, especially, were in favor of Sun because they believed that he stood for the rights of man and was opposed to oppression and cruelty, as shown in the policy of the Manchus.

In 1910 I was in Honolulu when Sun came there, and, hearing he was to be at the Fort Street Chinese Church, I went there to hear him and spoke with him. He called at my house soon after and we had a long talk. I asked him how the revolutionary movement was getting on and he said that the rising would occur the next year and that the plans were so well laid that this time he was sure of success. He told me that when last in China he could go about anywhere in the South for the soldiers were with him and were ready to join the revolutionists and that as he went about they even guarded him. He left Honolulu in 1910 and before he went away the Chinese gave him a farewell reception at which the Rev. Frank Damon presided, for he was in sympathy with the aims of Dr. Sun. I was present as a friend and marked the enthusiasm which was shown.[1]

Mr. Hori told the writer that he had formed a high opinion of Dr. Sun and admired his ability and his devotion to his principles, but did not think that Sun realized the difficulties which were before him in organizing the Republic of China if the Manchus were overthrown, as he believed would soon be the case. Sun appeared to think that if a republic were declared, evils would disappear and righteousness prevail. Hori had some doubts as to whether Sun was the man to develop a stable government, and whether the existing conditions of graft, "squeeze," jealousy, and political intrigue could be swept away suddenly. He referred to the fact that Japan had adopted modern methods gradually, and he questioned whether China with its illiteracy and ignorance was ready for a republican form of government. When he was told of a statement written by

[1] From an interview with the writer. Mr. Hori read it when written and indorsed it.

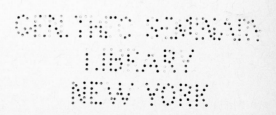

President Wilson that after mature study he had come to the conclusion that the same form of government was not suitable for all people, Mr. Hori said this was very true, but Sun did not seem to realize it. He had set his heart on having a republic and believed it the only remedy for existing evils.

In all that Mr. Hori saw of Sun, he believed him to be a sincere, high-minded, and honest man. He recognized the devotion of the leader to his people and his love of his native land, and agreed with his ideals—particularly that of enlightenment of China through education. He knew that Dr. Sun had attended Iolani, a church school, and had been graduated from a Christian medical college, and said that in many conversations with him, everything showed that he was in accord with Christian principles.

When Dr. Sun left Honolulu in 1910, he evidently did not want the public to know where he was going; if his destination had been known, the information would have been cabled at once to the Chinese Government. He did not succeed in concealing this, however, for a newspaper of the day published the story that Sun Yat Sen had gone on board the interisland steamer, *Claudine,* which was about to sail for Maui; but as soon as those who came to see him off had left, he quitted the steamer and boarded the *Mongolia,* which was about to depart for the Orient.[1] Nor was he able to conceal the fact of his arrival in Yokohama, for it was published that Sun Yat Sen had landed under the name of Aloha, and that in Japan he was going under the name of S. Takano.

While at Tokyo he was the guest of a friend expect-

---

[1] The *Honolulu Advertiser.*

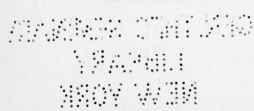

ing shortly to rent a house, but—his identity being discovered—he was compelled to leave the country. The Government of Japan evidently did not want to harbor the archrevolutionist, and sent him word to that effect. He left Yokohama for Singapore, where he had sought refuge before and where he was safe among his friends.

While Sun was traveling about, Gen. Wang Hing had started a revolt in Yamchow, and in 1910 there was an outbreak under a Manchu leader; but neither of these was of special significance. In the summer of 1911 Wang Hing was in Kwangtung, waiting for orders with a full knowledge that other provinces were prepared to rise when the word was given.

Meanwhile Sun had again gone to the United States, and was telling his friends that this time he was sure of success and that all would be ready in a few months. In the early months of 1911 he visited San Francisco, Seattle, Spokane, Kansas City, St. Louis, Chicago, and New York. In all of these places there were organized companies which had been drilled under the direction of Homer Lea. While this military training served to keep alive the men's interest in the revolution, it is doubtful whether many of them went back to fight in it, although a number returned to China after the overthrow of the Manchus to see whether there was anything for them to do.

While Sun was in America, news came that the Republic of China had been declared at Wuchang. He at once issued a statement addressed to the people of the United States, setting forth the principles and aims of the revolution, with the view of enlisting sympathy for the new Republic. He maintained that its government would be like that of the United States, the provinces having certain powers under the central authority. The press was very anxious to get a personal interview with him, but he managed to keep himself secreted in a hotel near Madison Square, New York. The Chinese who knew of his whereabouts would tell the reporters nothing. He took his meals with his old friend Tong Phong, from Hongkong, who at that time had a store near the hotel where Sun had a room. It was in the care of Tong Phong that a cablegram came announcing the premature outbreak in October, and insisting that he return to China at once.

He was to have sailed on the *Mauretania* but missed that steamer; and although his departure was delayed for two weeks, his identity was not discovered. At the end of that time he booked on another vessel, under an assumed name, and reaching England remained *incognito*.

He went direct to London and was again the guest of Dr. Cantlie, whom he told that he wanted to raise a loan of £500,000 sterling, in order to finance the work which yet had to be done. Sun never seems to have given up hope that he could borrow money in America or Europe, on the prospect of his success. It is believed that, besides the contributions from his countrymen, he received gifts from friends of other nationalities, but he found that capital is shy of making loans on political ventures. Before 1911, and even after that date, he had no practical ideas on the subject of loans from foreigners, which he sought to obtain on several occasions. As to his own countrymen, those who had wealth in China were not as a rule in sympathy with him because he disturbed business; and in lending money, while they are ready to assist relatives and friends, they are exceedingly shrewd and careful. He could obtain gifts but not loans.

While Sun was a guest of Dr. Cantlie, he received a cablegram addressed simply "Sun Wen, London," he having given that name at the cable office. Dr. Cantlie stated that this telegram announced his election as President of the Chinese Republic; but he was not elected to that office until January, 1912, when he was in Shanghai.

The outbreak of the revolution earlier than the time planned was the result of an accident. During the time that Sun had been abroad his agents had been busy everywhere, and at several places explosives were being manufactured. While they were waiting for word to come from headquarters to begin operations, a bomb exploded in a house in Hankow where the revolutionists had been making them. This aroused suspicion; the Imperial troops were called out; and the uprising followed. Rebel forces hastened north from the southern provinces; the revolt spread down the Yangtse River; and large bodies of the Imperial army joined the movement. When the southern provinces were in the hands of the insurgents, the Republic was proclaimed and Dr. Sun was requested by cable to return immediately.

There had not been much bloodshed in this revolution, in contrast with the Taiping Rebellion in which many millions lost their lives, or the Mohammedan uprising in 1857–74, in which millions more died. There had been some fighting at Sianfu, Wuchang, and Foochow, and a few thousand had been killed. Between the commencement of conflict at Wuchang on October 10 and the declaration of the Republic on December 2, 1911, eleven provinces had renounced allegiance to the

Manchu government. Then a conference of leaders was called and Sun was notified that he would be chosen the first president.

On leaving London, Sun assumed his official name, Sun Wen, the need of an *incognito* having passed. He went to Paris and at once hastened to Marseilles, thence by way of Suez to Singapore. There he received his first ovation from his countrymen; they hailed him as the liberator of China, and as he went from the ship a company of young girls strewed his path with flowers.

When he arrived at Hongkong he wrote a declaration of the intentions of the Chinese Republic, which he sent to the Department of State at Washington with the purpose of getting recognition by the United States as soon as possible. He knew that in the past Americans had been in favor of expressing their sympathy by recognizing republics.

Sun Yat Sen reached Shanghai two days after Christmas, and was received with enthusiasm as the man who was to be the head of the new government. It was firmly believed that the forces of the Republic were now of sufficient strength to march to Peking and expel the Manchus. Five days after landing at Shanghai, Sun Yat Sen was elected President of China, by the Assembly in session at Nanking, which had been selected as the future capital of the nation.

After years of plotting, strife, and danger, the village boy had come into power as the ruler of millions of people. The revolutionist who had been an outlaw, with a huge price set upon his head, was the chief of the Republic which he had done so much to found. But while he watched the exhibitions of joy by his countrymen, he knew that there was a mighty task before him. The

Manchus were still in Peking. They had to be expelled and order had to be restored. Time, wisdom, and patience, as well as statesmanship, were required to overcome the jealousy between north and south China, the intrigues of the war lords, and the system of graft and "squeeze" among the official class. From remarks that he made to friends, it would seem that he had doubts whether he was the man to meet these difficulties. He had been a successful revolutionist. Would he be a successful constructionist? That was the question which he had to face as he proceeded to Nanking.

## CHAPTER XIII

# Treachery and Disillusionment

## Sun Resigns from the Presidency. Yuan Shih
## Kai Becomes President and Plots in Vain
## To Make Himself Emperor. Sun
## Again a Fugitive

THE speedy success of the revolution of 1911 was due to the fact that Imperial forces joined the rebels. This had been brought about by systematic propaganda carried on for years. Following the war with Japan a great many students had been sent abroad for military training, most of them to Japan. Among these students constant work had been carried on by Sun and his agents; when they returned to China to take positions as officers in the Imperial army they were ready to turn over the troops, which they commanded, to the revolutionary cause when the outbreak occurred. Even before the accidental bursting of the bomb at Hankow, the government had been suspicious and had commenced to disarm the soldiers who were thought to be disaffected.

Yuan Shih Kai had been recalled from retirement and had been made commander of the Imperial army. When he recognized the strength and extent of the revolution, he concluded that the better plan was to come to some agreement with its leaders. Yuan Shih Kai was a crafty and able man. He had said that he did not believe that China was ready for a republican form of government and that he was in favor of a constitutional monarchy. It is evident from what followed that Yuan, on consultation with Sun, agreed to bring about the peaceful abdication of the Manchus and to accept the reform program, on condition that he should be the President of the Republic. Sun was to be elected the first president and then resign in favor of Yuan.

On January 1, 1912, Sun Yat Sen was elected President of the Republic of China by the Assembly, composed of leading men from the provinces which had joined in the revolution. A provisional constitution was set forth, and Sun, with his usual alacrity, sent a manifesto to the nations of the world relating the evils which had prevailed under the Manchu rule and maintaining that the only remedy was the establishment of a republic. He promised that all treaties made by the Powers with the Manchus would be continued, all concessions respected, and all property of foreigners protected, and that the aim would be the building up of a stable government, the elevation of the people, legislation for their welfare and prosperity, and maintenance of security and peace.

He resigned on February 12, 1912, because he believed it was the only way to get rid of the Manchus without further fighting. He had seen all his previous attempts to overthrow the Manchus fail, and he was unwilling to run the risk of being beaten again.

When his intention to resign was known cablegrams were sent to him from all parts of the world begging him to retain the office. His old and tried friends in Hawaii sent him messages protesting against such action, and those who were members of his household in Nanking pled with him, but it was of no avail. Among those of his household was Sun Fo, his son. He was a student at the University of California when he received word that his father was to be elected President, and he at once started for home. At Honolulu he was joined by the old friend of the family, Luke Chan, and twelve young men, all of whom had been educated abroad, most of them in California. To these had come the call to return to China and assist in the organization of the departments of the new government. They had with them the flag of the Republic of China which had been used at the time of the uprising of 1895. It had been designed by Luke Ho Tung who, as has been related, was captured and beheaded.

The first step of the Young China party had been to petition Peking to start agricultural schools. What had failed in 1894 might now be undertaken and Luke Chan had the promise of Dr. E. V. Wilcox of the United States Experiment Station in Hawaii to go to China to take charge of this work as soon as there was a stable government. The party of young men proceeded at once to Nanking, for on reaching China the news had been given them that Sun Yat Sen was President. Sun Fo and some of the party were quartered in the palace where the President resided, and they were amazed and distressed to learn that Sun Yat Sen intended to resign in favor of Yuan Shih Kai. All of the young Chinese who had gathered in Nanking, especially those who had been educated in America, were indignant at the idea. They had no confidence in any promises which Yuan had made.

The question of the resignation of President Sun came before the representatives of the revolted prov-

inces in January and was debated for days with great
earnestness. Those present were almost unanimously
opposed to it and showed a deep distrust of Yuan.
Every effort was made to get Sun to change his purpose,
but he was obdurate. He told the Assembly that Yuan
could secure the abdication of the Manchus readily and
that no one else could do it. This would be done peacefully. Any other plan would mean that they would have
to fight their way to Peking, and they had no money to
carry on a long campaign. When Sun's determination
was recognized as final, sorrow took the place of anger
and some gave way to despair. Gen. Wang Hing,[1]
who had so long and faithfully served the cause as commander of the revolutionary forces, wept bitterly, for
he had been emphatic in advocating a march to Peking.

This account of what took place in the Assembly and
in the residence of the President is from information
given by men who were actually present at the discussions and private conferences. It shows a greatness in
the character of Sun, that he put aside personal ambition and gain for what he believed to be best for the
country. He believed in the promises of Yuan to carry
out the republican program.

Persuaded by Yuan, the Manchus abdicated on February 12, 1912, and the new Empress Dowager, in the
name of the dynasty, issued an edict which was a
masterpiece as an illustration of saving what the Chinese call "face." A portion of it reads:

The majority of the people are in favor of a republic, such
being the general inclination, Heaven's ordinance may be di-

---

[1] Wang Hing is the Cantonese form for the name, appearing here
and elsewhere, which is more familiarly known in its Mandarin form,
Huang Hsing.

vined. How could I dare to disregard the wishes of millions
for the sake of the glory of one family? The Emperor and I
will retire into leisure and see the consummation of wise government. This will be excellent indeed.

When the abdication took place, Sun made a public
visit to the tombs of the Ming dynasty, and there paid
honor to the shades of the departed Chinese rulers. He
was following the ancient custom of expressing reverence for the dead, but he had a special purpose: He
wished to call the attention of the people to the fact
that China was again ruled by Chinese. By announcing
to the departed Mings that the rule of the Manchus was
at an end, he was telling the people in a dramatic way
that his national party had been successful.

The function over, the President went to his residence; there a reception was held at which he made an
address telling the people that Nanking was to be the
capital and that Yuan would soon come there to as-
sume his duties. In conclusion he said:

Yuan Shih Kai has given his adhesion to our cause and is at
one with our aspirations. He was our opponent yesterday, but
to-day he is our friend. When he comes he will receive the
welcome of a united people. When I retire to private life I
shall be a citizen as one of you, and shall try to forward to the
best of my ability the interests of the Republic. Long live the
Republic!

On February 13, 1912, Sun Yat Sen resigned, and
next day at his earnest solicitation, Yuan Shih Kai was
elected president by the Assembly. This was according
to the constitution, which followed the French system;
it was of course impossible at this time to get any direct
expression of the popular will.

It was important to get the Powers to recognize the

Republic, especially if loans were to be negotiated. At this time Prince Kuhio was delegate to the Congress of the United States from the Territory of Hawaii, and to him influential Chinese in Honolulu cabled asking his assistance in procuring recognition for the Republic of China. He took active steps, and the United States was the first nation to give the desired recognition.

At this time there came to Nanking a Frenchman, Fernand Farjenel, a professor at the Collège Libre des Sciences Sociales, of Paris. He was asked to look into the finance department of the government and found everything antiquated and chaotic; but when he suggested changes, he reported that those in charge were too ignorant to profit by his advice. He saw a good deal of Sun, being consulted by him and having long conversations with him both in his public capacity and in the privacy of his home. Like other foreigners who saw Sun at Nanking, he received a very different impression of the man from that he had been led to expect by reports about him. He found him well informed in the philosophy and theories of social reform, and wrote:

Of all the Chinese whom I have met he impresses me with his candor and honesty, his whole aspect being quite out of keeping with his reputation for duplicity, cunning, and treachery. His face is distinctly prepossessing and he made a most favorable impression on me.[1]

An American journalist long resident in China wrote:

He is notably honest, sincere, and of high purpose. He is a prophet honored in his own country. He trusted Yuan, and competent foreigners shared in his views.[2]

It had been agreed that on his resignation, Sun

[1] Fernand Farjenel, *Through the Chinese Revolution.*
[2] Frederick McCormick, *The Flowery Republic.*

## SUN YAT SEN AT THE MING TOMBS

The procession in February, 1912, when he went to announce to the shades of the former Chinese dynasty the expulsion of the Manchus and the establishment of the Republic of China.

should be appointed Director of Railroads. He desired the office because he knew that one cause of the backwardness of China was the lack of intercommunication and transportation. Outside of the treaty ports and their immediate surroundings, the roads were mere wheel-tracks; and of railroads there were only a few thousand miles. Sun was not an engineer and his idea of railroads was very crude. Trained men ridiculed his plans and said that he had, on paper, divided up the country into squares without regard to rivers or mountains. There was no money to build railroads, but as usual he thought he could get money from Europe; he had an interview with Farjenel about obtaining a loan from France, but was told that the French were not rash speculators.

The estimate of the character of Yuan Shih Kai formed by these same men was very different. Yuan belonged to the old order, Sun to the new. Yuan had been treacherous and cruel; but with his ideas of oriental despotism, his actions no doubt seemed to him as a necessary part of the functions of a ruler. He had swept away those who stood in the path of his ambitions. He had developed the Chinese army and given it order and discipline, and he had treated his men fairly. When he was in charge of affairs in Korea he had autocratic power and, according to all accounts, he used it in an unscrupulous and brutal way.

Sun must have known all this, and that was the reason that his followers could not understand why he trusted the word of Yuan. It was not long before he found out that his trust had been misplaced. One of the first indications was Yuan's excuses for not moving the capital to Nanking according to agreement. He said that a meeting of troops demanded his presence in Peking. A few months after his resignation, Sun was invited to visit Peking, and he was received there as if he had been a prince. After several interviews with Yuan, he was convinced that there was no intention on the part of the President to carry out reforms under the provisions of the constitution. Sun's suspicions were aroused. He knew that Yuan was a Chinese of the old style, who, in order to get rid of a possible trouble-maker, might imprison him and on some pretext have him beheaded. He left Peking secretly and returned to Nanking.

Yuan was short of money and was anxious to obtain a foreign loan. What funds there had been in the treasury had been used to pay off the Southern army and to add to the Northern forces. He managed to negotiate a loan of £25,000,000 sterling from a group of European financiers who acted with the consent of their governments.

This loan had been contracted without the consent of the Assembly, and was therefore contrary to the constitution. Upon learning what had been done, the Assembly declared the loan void. When it was discovered that the President was using the money to purchase arms from the Krupps, instead of applying it to internal improvements, the spirit of rebellion again flared up. Sun issued a statement accusing Yuan of being a tyrant. He begged the Powers to prevent the further advance of funds which, he was sure, would be used to put an end to the Republic and promote the ambitions of Yuan.

Early in May, 1913, Sun learned from friends in Peking that Yuan was laying plans to get rid of him. He could scarcely believe it when he heard on good authority that at a secret meeting of Yuan's Council he had been declared a traitor as had also Wu Ting Fang, and Dr. Lee, a leading revolutionist. Even then he did not think that the government would really try to arrest him. One day while in the yard in front of Dr. Lee's house, which was surrounded by a wall in the Chinese style, he and those with him heard a loud knocking at the gate. What followed can best be told in Sun's own words:

I recognized the voice of those in command outside the wall as that of Yi Ho, the brutal and unscrupulous hireling of the council police. I then realized that the information which we had received was true, and that if caught I should be rushed to Peking for secret trial and decapitation. Dr. Lee went to the gate to open it, but just before he did it he motioned me to leave. I knew the premises well and took what is known as the hill path to the rear. As I was leaving I could hear that Dr. Lee and the rest were buffeted and bound.

When I reached my house in Nanking before daylight the next morning, there was something which told me that it had been visited during the night, and I went to the house of a friend on the Honan Drive. There I learned that the previous afternoon my residence had been watched and my wife questioned by officers. I never was so mortified in my life, not even when held a prisoner in London. I was being hunted by the very government which I had helped to establish a few months before.

It probably will be denied that the foreign authorities refused me shelter. I made no application, but it is a fact that the head of the French police, and the head of the British service, sought me out during my stay and told me that I must take my chance if I remained. How did they know where I was? They knew that hired assassins would be after me day and night. Then I considered appealing to the United States Consul General, but of course I was not a citizen of America and could not legally claim protection. But the cry of the American Pretender was hurled against me.

For three weeks I tried to communicate with General Huang Hsing (Wang Hing in Cantonese), commander of the Southern army. I moved from house to house, and also at night made several trips to the city (Nanking), once in disguise I went to my own house and remained there till morning. On one occasion a drunken officer had come to my house, so my wife told me, and had roughly treated her and her two sisters, and pulled my sick daughter out of bed. Then with bayonets they destroyed the beds and the furniture. The chief threatened to send my wife to Peking unless she told them where I was, but on her knees she avowed that she did not know, which was true. I last saw my wife on June 13, 1913, she said, "Do not come again, go to Huang Hsing, do not be trapped here like a dog and be butchered."

I will not tell you how I got to Hongkong, and thence to Canton. I was a week on the trip and it cost me one hundred and thirty-five pounds sterling. The captain of the native steamer from Hongkong knew me well, for I had given him medical treatment at Macao and at Hongkong, and although he had never paid me anything yet he charged me $500.00 from Hongkong to the Pearl River. He was, I knew from his conversation, a supporter of Yuan Shih-kai, but I knew that I could trust him in a personal matter. He landed me at Go-lan and he secured a boatman to take me to Canton.

The captain of the steamer was not the only one who knew me and leered at me. He was the boss of the coolies and at Canton he informed the officials that I was in the city. I saw him once with an officer pass an office where I was resting. When I reached the camp of General Huang Hsing at Moochow, this fellow came up to me and wanted to shake my hand in the European fashion. This was after I had seen him in Canton with General Luang, the Governor General of the police. When he appeared at Moochow I denounced him, and by order of Huang Hsing he was cut in many pieces.

I wanted to see my family and General Huang Hsing volunteered to risk sending word and financial assistance and to get a return message. For several days before our departure we had gone about the city in the poorest garb and lived among the meanest class on the river, and at times I had a creepy feeling because of the big reward offered for my capture. General Huang and I left the city in the same house-junk, but we were supposed never to have met before. He paid five Canton taels ($3.00) for his fare and I gave four dollars, Mexican, and a package of groceries, some eight or nine pounds of provisions which I had been carrying in an old shirt for several days. Of course we had funds on our persons to take us to America, if we decided to go, but it would have courted death to let the boatman know this.

From He Ling, General Huang secured passage on a steamer to Hongkong, while I went to Macao in a fishing boat. After twelve days I was happy to land at Moji (in Japan) and was delighted to learn that General Huang had done all that he had promised and he had landed at Nagasaki five days before me. We met at the Inland Sea Hotel, a place both of us knew when we had been hunted fugitives, and where we had agreed to meet.

From Nagasaki Sun Yat Sen wrote to Yuan Shih Kai that he was a traitor to his country, and that as he (Sun) had risen to overthrow the Manchus, so he would rise against Yuan.

Sun Yat Sen was again an exile. Once more he had failed in carrying out his plans for the unification of China under a republic. Many of the Progressive party were wholly discouraged and thought it would be better to conform to existing conditions. But Sun still believed in the people and set to work planning and plotting for the future.

After he left China an abortive attempt at rebellion had occurred at Nanking in July, 1913, but it was crushed by relentless methods similar to those the Manchus had used. Sun knew that it was useless to attempt to overthrow Yuan at that time, for the republican organization had been abandoned after the Manchu abdication. He remained in Japan for a few months and then moved to Shanghai, where he lived in the French Concession. There he waited for a propitious time for another uprising in favor of constitutional government.

Yuan, from the day of his election, had set to work to strengthen the central government and augment his own power. Despite his promises to make Nanking the capital, he retained Peking as the seat of government. There were too many sympathizers with Sun at Nanking, and besides, the Legations were in Peking and prestige would be lost if a removal were made from a city so long associated with Chinese greatness. Yuan was worried by what he believed was the encroachment of Japan, and he was dubious about the conduct of Russia on the north. He believed that China needed a strong man to manage affairs at home and abroad.

In October, 1913, he arranged to get the Assembly to elect him President for five years. Then by getting rid of the radical members and dismissing the Provincial Councils, he made himself virtually dictator. In 1914 he promulgated a revised constitution which lengthened the term of President to ten years and practically gave him the power to appoint his successor. In 1915 the military chiefs expressed their opinion in favor of Yuan declaring himself Emperor. Then Yuan managed to have petitions sent to him from all parts of the country begging him to abolish the republic and establish a constitutional monarchy.

At this time Yuan's adviser on governmental affairs was the American Dr. F. J. Goodnow, who had pursued his constitutional studies in Germany. This may have influenced his judgment in the long argument which he wrote, at the request of the President, advocating a monarchical form of government as better suited for China than a republican system.

A long reply to Dr. Goodnow was published by Kang Yu Wei who was the man who had influenced the Emperor Kuang Hsu in 1898 to issue the reform edicts. But Yuan had made up his mind and, early in 1916, he issued a proclamation that acceding to the will of the people and loving his country, he declared himself Emperor, the first of a new dynasty.

As soon as this was done the south and west were in a ferment of excitement. Yunnan threatened to revolt. Delegates of the southern provinces met in Canton, formed a confederacy, and seceded. Szechuan declared against Yuan. When he heard of it he became frantic with rage; and going into the room where his favorite concubine lay with her newborn baby, he drew his sword and slew them both. Why he did this is a mystery, but he may have had in mind that this child was to succeed him and he saw that the end of his ambitious schemes had come. On March 22, after only a few weeks as Emperor, he issued a decree abrogating the Empire and restoring the Republic. There is no doubt that bitter disappointment and financial difficulties, which had increased with the southern revolt, hastened his death on June 1, 1916.

The Vice-President, Li Yuan Hung, succeeded Yuan. He had refused to favor the monarchy; and on his accession, those who had plotted to establish it fled to escape arrest.

During these three years, from 1913 to 1916, Sun had remained most of the time in Shanghai. He had a good house and lived well, partly in Chinese and partly in European style both as to food and dress. He enter-

tained guests, though not lavishly, being restrained in
his habits and an abstainer from the use of wine and
tobacco. People have inquired as to the sources of his
income at this time. An American who was employed
then in the Shanghai Post Office, later told the writer
that no less than 25,000 registered letters addressed to
Sun came during this period. These arrived from all
parts of the world—America, Australia, Singapore, and
elsewhere—and presumably contained money. Some
money was sent from Honolulu, for receipts are shown
there for sums which run to a total of over $15,000.
These remittances were sent by Luke Chan and the receipts were signed by Sun Wen and his treasurer.
Rumors were always current among his opponents that
Sun was obtaining money from those who wanted to
gain his influence. The custom among Chinese officials
of making money out of their positions was so universal
that his enemies could not imagine that he had not been
getting rich out of his revolutionary schemes.

Men who knew Sun well, both Chinese and foreigners, had a different opinion of him, and believed
him to be both honest and unselfish. They cite the fact
that he gave up the office of Director of Railroads, with
its salary of £40,000 a year, rather than be untrue to
republican principles. There is no doubt that he received money from his sympathizers while he was in
Shanghai, but he was still the leader of the Progressives
and was planning all the time to bring about another
uprising, when, in his judgment, it was likely to be
successful.

In interviews which he gave in Shanghai it was
evident that, while hopeful, yet he had come to believe
that no great change would come to China for a long

time. He was inclined to look to Japan for help in the development of the country, because the Japanese understood the Chinese better than Europeans and Americans did. He was in correspondence with prominent Japanese and this probably gave rise to the report that he was receiving financial aid from them. What gave him encouragement was that he saw a glimmer of the spread of a national spirit in China, although he must have known that this was confined almost entirely to the students. But it was true that they greatly influenced those with whom they came in contact, for the Chinese have a profound respect for the educated man. Sun went so far as to say that he might not live to see any radical change, but he was sure it would come some day. Meanwhile all interested must continue the work of agitation, and give instruction as to organization and the conduct of public affairs.

Foreigners who conversed with him had the opinion that he did not realize the danger of depending too much on Japan. He favored getting Japanese to come to China to instruct the people. When it was pointed out to him that such a peaceful penetration might be dangerous to the future of the country, he scoffed at the thought of it. He was looking for help from some foreign nation, and the Japanese would no doubt have been glad to have made favorable terms with him if he had possessed power to make an agreement. In this respect they were not different from other nations, any one of which would have been eager for the opportunity to direct Chinese affairs.

All that Sun said and did while he was in Shanghai, at this time and later, plainly showed that he never fully gauged the obstacles in the way of the establishment of a republic. Many Chinese who were his supporters came to see that the ignorance of the masses, the lack of any comprehension of representative government, and the clinging to ancient methods must be overcome before a real republic can be in practical operation.

Sun Yat Sen in 1916 did realize, in a measure, that it is one thing to overthrow, but another matter to build up. It was this problem that he had to face when, in 1917, the southern provinces revolted and he returned to Canton to take part in the administration of affairs.

## CHAPTER XIV

# Sun Yat Sen and His Family

## His Break with His Brother and His First Wife.
## His Second Marriage

RELATIONS between Sun Yat Sen and his family require discussion here because of an event which occurred while he was in Shanghai in 1915. The account goes back to 1896, and forward until Sun went to Peking shortly before his death. It is a connected story, and all of it has to do with Sun's second marriage to Miss Sung Hing Ling.

Ah Mi, as the elder brother of Sun Yat Sen was always called in Hawaii, became very prosperous as the years passed. After he had disposed of his interests in Honolulu and in the country near by, he leased a large tract of land on the island of Maui, on the slopes of Haleakala, an extinct volcano, ten thousand feet high, and there he raised cattle. This business, together with a store at Kahului, the seaport of the east side of the island, made him a rich man for those times. He was well known by the Chinese and other races as a careful and honorable business man.

His mother had lived with him since 1896, as had also the wife of his brother, Dr. Sun, and her three children. Of course it was impossible for Sun's wife to accompany him as he traveled about the world arousing his countrymen against the Manchu rule and preaching the doctrine of progress for China; but during his frequent visits to the Hawaiian Islands, he would go to Maui to see his family.

Time had changed Ah Mi's attitude toward his younger brother; and although he was not in sympathy with his religious views, he was with him heart and soul in his hatred of the Manchus and in his desire for the enlightenment of China.

When Sun was in Hawaii in 1896, he was on his way to the mainland of the United States and later to England. As soon as Ah Mi heard of his brother's capture and escape in London, like all other Chinese in Hawaii he was greatly interested; and when he learned that the servant of the Legation, who had helped his brother to escape, had lost his position, he sent Sun Yat Sen money to pay the man what he considered a debt of gratitude. Chinese in Honolulu, who knew of the circumstance, say that the amount was several thousand dollars. With the strong family feeling the Chinese have, to help his brother in difficulty was the natural thing to do.

Residence in Hawaii had evidently modified his antipathy to the Christian religion, or at least toward Christians. At the end of the nineteenth and the beginning of the twentieth century, a large number of Chinese farmers had leased land in the neighborhood of Ah Mi's ranch, on which they raised corn and other crops. Among these were many earnest Christians, and with them he was on good terms. On one occasion Bishop Alfred Willis, who had been Sun Yat Sen's teacher, went on a visit to members of his diocese who lived on the mountain, and he was entertained by Ah Mi. The Bishop had with him, as his interpreter, a young man named Yap See Yung; he had been a pupil at Iolani School, and was among the youths who were at the first meeting of the revolutionists in Honolulu and took the oath to further the cause which Dr. Sun presented so forcibly.

As Sun continued his revolutionary activities, Ah Mi contributed most generously to the expenses of the movement, sending his brother thousands of dollars at a time. Evidently proud of him, for his name was in the mouth of everyone, Ah Mi probably looked forward to some office under him when success should come to the revolution, to achieve which he was anxious to help in every way possible. In 1909 he sold out his large interests on Maui and went to China, taking up his residence at Kowloon, across the bay from Hongkong, which is British territory. As a brother of the archrevolutionist he dared not trust himself on Chinese soil, and besides, like many Chinese who had made money abroad and returned home, he felt safer on land controlled by foreigners.

He had not been long at Kowloon before it was known that his house was the meeting place of the sympathizers with the revolution; and the British authorities, learning of this, informed him that his presence was undesirable and advised or ordered him to depart. He then went to Kwangchau-wan, a French possession, where he ostensibly operated a drug store; really it was the headquarters of Sun's followers in that territory. He did not remain there long, for in 1912, when his brother was elected President of the Republic of China, he moved to Macao, where he would be near Canton and ready to take advantage of any opportunity that might come his way.

During the troublous time following the flight of Dr. Sun from Nanking, Ah Mi found the situation difficult.

His fortune had been spent to promote the revolution and his brother was an exile. All he could do was to wait until the tide changed, which his hopeful brother was sure would happen in due time.

When Sun came to Canton and was in power, Ah Mi had the ambition to become Governor of the province of Kwangtung, and expected the office as a reward for the aid he had given to his party. When Dr. Sun told him plainly that he did not have the ability to fill the position properly, Ah Mi became angry and said that he wanted back the money that he had advanced. Hot words passed between them, and the end was that Dr. Sun said he would give him a certain sum, amounting to about $20,000. This was a repayment of what Ah Mi considered a loan to be reimbursed when the Republic was established. A large part of this sum was spent in the purchase of a very fine house in Macao, which had been erected by a judge. Those who have seen it describe it as palatial and beyond the means of Ah Mi to maintain.

When Ah Mi returned to China from Hawaii in 1909, Sun Yat Sen's wife was with his party, and after her husband was elected president she went to Nanking. Then he fled from Yuan Shih Kai, and she went to Macao, where she still lives. She became a convert to the Christian religion; and after a while was given occupation by one of the missions as a Bible woman, with the duty to go into Chinese homes to teach the Gospel to the women of the household, custom preventing a man from doing such work.

The reason that she did not live with her husband when he returned as Director of the Canton Government in 1916, and later when he was President of the South, involves a chapter in the life of Sun Yat Sen upon which Chinese, whether Confucian or Christian, look with regret and disfavor.

When Sun was in Shanghai, in the early part of 1915, he had as his secretary Miss Sung Hing Ling. She was an attractive young woman who had been educated in America, and is said to have been a graduate of Wesleyan College, Macon, Georgia. She was an ardent sympathizer with the revolution and a great admirer of Dr. Sun. On the one hand was a wife who was of the old style, from whom his protracted wanderings had kept him apart most of the time for twenty years; and on the other, a modern woman, well educated, with whom he was daily associated in helpful relationship.

A Chinese man,[1] a great friend of Sun's, after talking over with others the rumor that their leader was intending to put away his wife and marry his secretary, went to him, intending to urge him not to take the step. Sun's friends knew how strongly he had expressed himself against the practice of taking a concubine; and to get rid, by any method, of his wife—the mother of his children, who had been faithful to him, and had endured hardships due to his revolutionary activities— was contrary to Chinese ethics. Accordingly, Sun's friend called to offer advice; but when they were together his courage failed and he remained silent. When Dr. Sun asked him why he was so gloomy, he made an excuse of not feeling well and left, as he said, with a lump in his throat.

According to a report, Sun's wife went to Japan on

[1] Chang Chau.

the invitation of her husband and there gave her consent to a separation. What took place is not exactly known, though what was said to be her statement was published. It was reported that they were divorced, but many Chinese do not see how this could be done. It is stated that Dr. Sun married Miss Sung Hing Ling[1] in Japan on October 25, 1915.

The marriage was widely discussed by his friends and followers in China and Hawaii, who deeply regretted his action. When Dr. Sun went to Peking with his second wife—for wife he always called her—the foreign ladies at first received her graciously; but when they were made aware of her status, they dropped her, evidently not considering her his wife. Without any intention of condoning Sun's conduct, in considering the whole matter one must admit that what he did was not different from, and certainly not worse than, what is done by thousands of Americans. One can comprehend, from the standpoint of human nature, how easy it was for him to fall in love with this educated and refined woman who understood him and his aims; but from the point of view of Chinese custom and ethics, his action was wrong. With his professed religious belief, he ought to have had respect for the Christian ideals of marriage. But the facts, as far as they could be ascertained, show that his action was not essentially different from that of thousands of men and women in Christian America.

Sun's second wife, after the death of her husband, was for some time a leader in the councils of the Nationalists. She declared her intention of devoting herself

[1] Her name is here given as Dr. Sun spelled it. Some put her surname last and spell it "Soong."

## SUN YAT SEN AND SUNG HING LING

This photograph of the revolutionary leader with his second wife was taken in 1915.

to the cause to which Sun had given his entire thought and strength. Later she fell out with those in power, declaring that they were not following out the principles which Sun had advocated.

## CHAPTER XV

# A Fresh Beginning in Canton

The Conflict of South and North China. Sun's
Relations with Japan and Soviet Russia,
and Troubles with the Powers

WHEN the southern provinces were in revolt
in 1916, demanding a return to the provisional constitution, Sun Yat Sen returned to
Canton and became the leading member of the Administrative Council. In this office he tried earnestly to
promote good government, to maintain order, to suppress graft, and to improve the city.

In 1917, the Parliament at Peking having been dissolved, Sun induced a number of the southern delegates
to organize an opposition government at Canton. He
convinced them that the North was antagonistic to republican principles, and that the South must stand firm
or the work of the revolution would be undone. The
southern government was organized and Sun, as its
head, was given the title of Generalissimo. It was not
long before circumstances demanded a strong assertion
of power, and Sun, for a while, was virtually dictator.
Many longed for the openness of the old days. They
had wanted a republic, but they had not realized that
it meant such sweeping reforms as were taking place.
The struggle between the old and the new was proceeding in Canton and in China at large.

Sun was made to realize as never before that it was much easier to arouse enthusiasm for the revolution and the Republic than it was to manage the leaders and to change the ideas of government, the inheritance of centuries, with the accompanying corruption, to which the older Chinese clung. On the other hand, the younger men, educated abroad, wanted to rush ahead too rapidly. As Sun said, they did not understand their own country and its people. The *tuchuns* or war lords could not be depended on; they would take one side or the other, as they judged their selfish interests would be served, making alliances with brigands or hiring mercenaries in order to further their ends.

The successors of Yuan Shih Kai were not strong men and they could not pacify the South; yet, amid all the turmoil and strife, people went on with their business, foreign trade increased, and the customs, the salt tax, and the postal service were carried on as usual. No doubt this was because foreigners were at the head of these departments.

In the early part of 1917 the question arose whether China should take part in the World War. Feng Kuo Chang became President in July, and upon him centered the pressure that for months had been brought to bear upon the Peking government to declare war against Germany. Sun was very much opposed to the policy. With him were other leaders, such as Kang Yu Wei, the reformer of 1898, who had held to his views for twenty years.

As early as March 7, 1915, Sun had written an open letter to Lloyd George, from which the following is taken:

## SUN YAT SEN AS GENERALISSIMO

This photograph was taken while he was at the head of the Canton administration in 1917.

. . . I have been approached by prominent Englishmen to consider the question of China joining the Allies. After careful study I come to the conclusion that it would be disastrous to both countries should China break her neutrality. For China is yet an infant Republic, and as a nation, she may be likened to a sick man just entering the hospital of constitutionalism. Unable to take care of herself at this stage, she needs careful nursing and support. Therefore China can not be regarded as an organized country. She is held intact only by custom and sentiment of a peace-loving people. But at once, should there arise discord, general anarchy would result. . . . Should China enter the war, it would prove dangerous to her national life, and injurious to the prestige of England in the Far East. The mere desire to get China to join the Allies, is to Chinese minds a confession of the Allies' inability to cope with Germany. . . . Already the question has raised bitter dissension among our statesmen. Discord may arouse anarchism, which will arouse the two strong but perilous elements in China, the anti-foreign fanatics and Mohammedans. [There were millions of these in the northwestern provinces.]

In 1915 Japan presented the Twenty-one Demands, which would have made China almost the vassal of the Island Empire. The United States Minister to China, Paul S. Reinsch, was greatly disappointed at the action of the Japanese. In Peking the officials told him that circumstances forced them to be friendly with Japan; they claimed to have proof that Sun Yat Sen, in the South, had assured that country more extensive rights of military and administrative supervision than the North had done.[1] No follower of Sun would believe this accusation. He loved his country, and he was too clever and too astute to hand it over to Japan, much as he might desire her aid in modernizing and unifying his distracted land.

[1] Paul S. Reinsch, *An American Diplomat in China.*

Sun Yat Sen was very anxious that the truth about China should be known to the world. Feeling desperate as he realized the disturbed condition of the country, he wrote to Reinsch:

Through you alone will the President and the people of the United States see the true state of affairs in China. Your responsibility is indeed great. Whether democracy or militarism triumph in China depends upon your Excellency's support of our helpless people at this stage.

Early in 1918 Sun realized that it was hopeless to make a pretense of carrying on a government at Canton, when there was no territory over which it had any sort of jurisdiction. He was forced to leave that city, and went again to Shanghai. Still he sent a message to his adherents: "Preach the gospel of justice and lead the people to righteousness." When the message reached his friends in Honolulu they were reminded of the motto inscribed on the coat of arms of Hawaii, the translation of which is, "The life of a land is established in righteousness." With it, no doubt, Sun was familiar.

In Shanghai, Sun was not idle, and to interviewers he complained that the South was not recognized by the Powers. He was busy in the preparation of an elaborate scheme which he called *The International Development of China*. It was submitted to the representatives of the Powers in China in March, 1919, and sent out to the various countries. It was an extraordinary compilation of the needs of China as they appeared to him, dealing with railroads, canals, harbors, and industries of different kinds, all of which he wanted financed by an agreement among the nations. His ideas, when they were published two years later in America, filled a book of 265 pages. First, he wanted the Powers to agree to form an international organization, and to have the men who had been leaders in war work make plans for and carry out the work. Second, these leaders must coöperate with the Chinese and gain their enthusiastic support. Third, the Powers must contract with the Chinese Government. After giving details of his stupendous program, he said, "The goal of material progress is not private profit but public profit." The profits of the complicated scheme should, he said, go first for interest, then to give high wages, and third to improve and extend production; the balance should be used to reduce the prices of all commodities.

Thus, all will enjoy, in the same degree, the fruits of a modern civilization. . . . In a nutshell it is my idea to make capitalism create socialism in China, so that those two economic forces of human evolution will work side by side in future civilization.

Many to whom this plan was sent made no reply, but Reinsch, the United States Minister, who was shortly to leave China, wrote a kindly answer; he rather liked Sun and wished to be courteous. He wrote:

I believe that at all times we should keep in mind the fact that we are not dealing with a new country, but with one in which social arrangements are exceedingly intricate, and where a long tested system of agriculture and industrial organization exists. . . . It is, to my mind, most important that the transition to new methods should not be sudden, but that the old values should be gradually transmitted.[1]

Sun never grasped the principles set forth by Reinsch; he seemed always to think that it was possible to set aside the customs of ages, by a formula on paper.

Among those who sent a reply was William C. Red-

[1] Paul S. Reinsch, *An American Diplomat in China,* p. 380.

field, Secretary of the Department of Commerce at Washington. He said:

The plans which you propose are so complex and extensive, that it will take years to work them out in detail. You doubtless are fully aware that it would take billions of dollars to carry out even a small portion of your proposals, and that most of them would not be able to pay interest charges and expenses for some years; . . . the revenues of the Chinese Republic are already too heavily burdened with the interest charges on existing Government loans to warrant further charges, and hence it would seem necessary to limit the projects to those which seem to be sufficiently remunerative to attract private capital.[1]

Other letters were brief and hinted at difficulties. They were all addressed to Sun at 29 Rue Molière, in the French Concession at Shanghai. This house had been given him by some of the patriotic Chinese living abroad, and more than once it had been mortgaged when funds were needed for the cause.

When Chinese overseas who were possessed of means knew of the plans for the development of China proposed by Dr. Sun, some of them were willing to devote their fortunes to promote their furtherance if there was a reasonable chance of success. In 1920, Sun went to Japan to investigate shipbuilding and to visit the government dockyards. A number of friends met him at Nagasaki, among them was his old schoolmate, C. K. Ai, who was interested in the project of reclaiming lands in the Yangtse Valley. But he and the others recognized the fact that until there was a stable government, nothing could be done.

At Shanghai, besides being engaged in publishing his

[1] Sun Yat Sen, *The International Development of China*, Appendix III.

## CHINESE REVOLUTIONISTS IN JAPAN

The photograph was taken during a conference at Nagasaki in 1920. First row: second from left, C. K. Ai of Honolulu; fourth from left, Sun Yat Sen.

plans for the development of China, Sun was plotting to regain power in Canton. Under General Chen he was organizing an army in Fukien, the purpose being to get that province to join forces with those favorable to his interests in the province of Kwangtung and to drive the Kwangsi party, which had resisted him, out of Canton. He believed that if he should regain control, a military expedition could be sent to the north; and with the success which he expected, he could command national respect and international recognition. After the usual plotting and intrigue, the followers of Sun gained the ascendancy in Canton, and then what was called the Southern Parliament met and elected him President of the Republic. On May 5, 1921, he was inaugurated. But General Chen and many influential citizens of Canton did not favor his election and never gave him genuine support, so that soon trouble was brewing for the new President.

When Sun took office, he at once began to devise plans for a military expedition to the north, for he believed there was no possibility of effecting the unity of China by negotiation. He was at once hampered by serious local troubles, the city and surrounding country were in such a disturbed condition that his powers were circumscribed in every direction. He had enemies in the south and foes in the north. Jealousy, suspicion, and intrigue prevailed everywhere.

Foreigners suggested to him that it would perhaps be the best arrangement if there should be a division of China into a northern and southern confederacy. They pointed out that if the country were divided in this way by agreement between the North and South, both divisions would be recognized by the Powers. Sun would not consider such a plan for a moment; he was sure the whole people would be opposed to it. Against it he urged the racial unity of the Chinese, the long history of China with the same racial culture, the same ethical system, the same customs and traditions. It was true that many dialects were spoken, but all these belonged to a common root language, and educated men were able to communicate with each other by means of the system of characters common to all. Sun agreed with those who advocated the teaching of Mandarin in all the higher schools, in the hope that many dialects would in time die out. Before his death he was interested in the work of the Progressives who began what was called mass education, with the purpose of overcoming illiteracy and furthering a national spirit.

During 1921 Gen. Wu Pei Fu of the North expressed a desire to unite the country under a constitutional government. He put himself in friendly communication with Sun and an attempt was made to arrange for a conference. After some correspondence the plan fell through, and Sun issued a denunciation of the President and the Peking government.

In the summer of 1921 serious troubles arose in Canton, due to differences between President Sun and Gen. Chen Chiung Ming. This was the man who had been appointed by Sun to try to bring the province of Fukien into line with the South; he was the commander of the southern forces. When Sun had ordered the expedition to start for the northern campaign, Chen had made the objection that the army was not ready. Sun insisted on an advance, but after a few minor successes, the whole movement resulted in a dismal failure. Chen claimed that Sun had not supported him as he should have done, a quarrel ensued, and Chen marched his troops to Canton and drove the President out of the city. Sun took refuge on a British gunboat and was taken to Hongkong, where he met a hostile attitude. Mrs. Sun had a narrow escape from capture. On June 6, at two o'clock in the morning, Sun went to her room and told her to get up and leave the house, as the troops under Chen were looting the city. She insisted that she felt quite safe in the palace and would remain there. Sun left a guard of fifty men in the palace yard and made for the river. Before long, Chen's soldiers came and fired on the guard with a machine gun, from the roof of a house near by. Realizing the danger of the situation Madam Sun and two guards escaped by crawling across a footbridge and succeeded in reaching the outskirts of the city where she sought refuge in a farmhouse. There she disguised herself as a countrywoman and made her way to the Canton Christian College. Without further difficulty, she then joined her husband on the British gunboat and went with him to Shanghai.

While Sun was at Shanghai at this time, the Peking government again tried to secure his coöperation in order that there might be an understanding and peace. These negotiations continued from the last part of 1922 to the early months of 1923. It appears that Sun did his best to bring about an amicable arrangement. At his earnest solicitation the members of the Parliament, who had left Peking six years before, returned to see what could be done. When they met they found that the northern members had not changed their ideas; so they returned home.

During the period of these conferences, a most important thing happened which had far-reaching conse-

quences. After the World War many Russians had arrived in Shanghai, and Sun came in touch with them. In
January, 1923, he met the Soviet representative, Adoff
Ioffe, and from that time had many conversations with
him. It was rumored that Sun was becoming a convert
to the Soviet system; the truth is that he was anxious to
get help from any possible quarter. He knew that the
Chinese social organization did not offer a suitable soil
for the growth of Soviet ideas, yet he was quite willing
to accept advice and listen with appreciation to promises
of financial assistance.

In order to allay the suspicion of foreigners, Sun and
Ioffe issued a joint statement to the press:

> Dr. Sun holds that the communistic order, or even the
> Soviet system, can not actually be introduced into China be-
> cause there do not exist here the conditions for the successful
> establishment of communism or sovietism. This view is en-
> tirely shared by Mr. Ioffe, who is further of the opinion that
> the paramount and most pressing Chinese problem is to
> achieve national unification and attain full independence. And
> regarding this great task, he has assured Dr. Sun that China
> has the earnest sympathy of the Russian people, and can count
> on the support of Russia.

This was the beginning of the great influence which
the Russians acquired in the affairs of Canton and
southern China.

In order to regain power in Canton, Sun and his party
engaged mercenaries from the provinces of Yunnan
and Kwangsi, and by their aid in February, 1923, the
way was opened for him to return to that city. Calling
at Hongkong on his way there, he was surprised to
find that the attitude of the press and people had
changed; he was received with a cordiality which

elicited wide comment. It was now believed that he was the strongest man in the South, and was more likely than anyone else to be able to straighten out the chaotic state of affairs. There was also another reason: Sun had been approaching British officials on the subject of amicable arrangements, and it was good policy on both sides to be friendly. Great Britain's interests in China were immense, far exceeding those of any other nation. In Peking was the only government that could be recognized; and yet the British authorities at Hongkong, because of business relations with Canton, were obliged to have all kinds of semiofficial dealings with Sun and his government, although he was a rebel.

In Canton as President of the South again, Sun was at once harassed by trying difficulties. The Yunnanese mercenaries, by whose aid General Chen had been driven out, were a turbulent lot and would not obey orders. When he had been in power in 1921–22, he had suppressed the gambling houses in Canton, but when Chen's troops were in the city they were reopened. Desperate for want of funds with which to pay the soldiers, Sun had allowed them to stay open under a high tax. He knew that there would be mutiny if the troops were not paid, and before long this was the case.

In the midst of these disturbances, in August, 1923, Michael Borodin arrived from Moscow. He came by invitation of Sun and by appointment of the Soviet Government, to act as adviser to the government of the South. Before he had returned to China in 1911, Sun had met Chicherin, the Russian revolutionist. They were both exiles at the time, and it was but natural that they should have exchanged views. They kept up a correspondence at intervals; and in 1920, when both of them

had seen their emperors dethroned, Chicherin wrote
to Sun from Russia telling him of his hope to spread
Sovietism in other countries. In this letter, written in
English, the Russian said, "Your country advances now
resolutely, your people enter consciously the path of
struggle against the world-suppressing yoke of im-
perialism." His closing words were: "Trade relations
must be taken up with us immediately. No opportunity
must be lost. Let China enter resolutely the path of
good friendship with us."

Two years after the receipt of this letter, Sun met
Ioffe in Shanghai, and, as has been shown, obtained
promises of assistance from him. Six months later, Boro-
din arrived in Canton. At first his salary was paid from
Moscow, but later it was assumed by the southern
Chinese government.

Sun's private secretary at this time was Eugene Chen,
who afterward became very influential in the Nationalist movement. He was born in the West Indies and was
not of pure Chinese blood. He had been educated in
England, but was a radical with antiforeign feelings
and in sympathy with the principles of the Russians.
Chen was present when Sun had his first interview with
Borodin, who was appointed high adviser of the President. Chen assumed that Sun had committed himself to
the Soviet doctrine, and said that the appointment was
made after deliberate consideration. From this time
Borodin was virtually the prime minister of the Republic of the South. Up to the time of his death, Sun im-
plicitly believed in the ability and loyalty of Borodin
and of the other Russians who came to work under his
direction.

Sun saw that without help he could never carry

through his ideas. He still believed in the plan set forth in his book, *The International Development of China,* and he knew that this could not even be commenced without the assistance of foreigners. America and Great Britain would do nothing, and he turned to Russia where there was promise of sympathy and financial coöperation. This was the positive statement of Eugene Chen.

When it was known in the treaty ports that Sun had entered into an agreement with the Russians, there was great alarm; the Soviet authorities announced that they were ready to abolish all unequal treaties. Borodin, within a month after his arrival, advised Sun to request the customs officials to turn over to the southern government the surplus amount received from duties collected in the Kwangtung Province. The customs service was managed for the Peking government by foreigners under the direction of a British subject, and the first charge on receipts was the payment of the interest on foreign loans, pledged according to agreement with the Government of China.

No reply was made to Sun's request; and in December he wrote threatening to seize the customhouses. Then the Treaty Powers sent a refusal and dispatched to Canton an international fleet of gunboats under the flags of the United States, Great Britain, France, Italy, Portugal, and Japan. To grant the request would have been a kind of recognition of a rebel government and a disregard of agreements made with Peking. Sun seems never to have grasped this. It was hard for him to see money collected in his province sent to the North to assist his enemies and, as he declared, to strike at republican principles.

The action of the Powers stirred up the greatest antipathy to foreign domination, and strengthened Russian influence. It was the general opinion, then and later, that Borodin was doing his best to injure Great Britain. Then and in the years that followed, boycotts and strikes wrought great harm to British interests, but they also caused immense loss to Chinese merchants and to the laboring classes.

In an address at a public meeting in the Canton Y.M.C.A., delivered on December 31, 1923, Sun said: "We no longer look to the western powers. Our faces are turned towards Russia." In June of the next year there were thirty-four Soviet agents assisting in the Canton government; of these, thirty were military experts, for Sun was preparing for another advance to the north. In 1924, he founded the Whampoa Military Academy, under the advice of Borodin, and Russian instructors trained men in modern methods of warfare. So a corps of cadets was formed, from which an efficient army was developed.

The North also had foreign assistants, political, financial, and military. According to the Chinese Year Book, there were attached to the Peking government at this time six American, four Japanese, two British, one Belgian, and two French advisers. Besides these there were one hundred and twenty-one foreign employees in the Post Office, sixty in the Salt Administration, and nearly one thousand in the Customs Service.

As the national consciousness grew, there was an intense feeling that China should be for the Chinese. Sun complained that foreigners at the head of departments had not trained Chinese for the high positions, but had used them only in the lower places.

Sun had not turned to the Russians without having tried other sources, as has been shown; even after his conferences with them he had been ready to accept aid from others. In 1923, when the American Minister to Peking, Jacob Gould Schurman, visited Canton, Sun questioned him as to the willingness of the Powers to bring about a joint intervention; as he frankly admitted, he believed that no man and no faction in China could bring peace to his distracted country. Schurman could give him no encouragement as to the possibility of action from outside.

It was reported, but Chinese think it incredible, that shortly before his death Sun made one more attempt for active intervention as the only means to bring about peace. He even proposed, it was said, that the Treaty Powers, under the leadership of the United States and Great Britain, should come into China, garrison the provincial capitals, take over the government, send out experts and administrators, and govern China for four years, inculcating order and efficiency, and then retire and turn over the government to responsible officials whom they had trained. It was also said that Sun promised, if they would accept his plan, to devote the rest of his life to further it. It is certain that Sun longed for peace, provided that it would not mean the division of the country. His hopes for the regeneration of his country by the overthrow of the Manchus had not been realized. He had failed to accomplish what was in his heart. He saw troublous times ahead, and he was a sick man.

## CHAPTER XVI

# The Last Years

Disorders in the South. The Death and Burial of
Sun Yat Sen. His Will and the Influence
of His Memory

THE closing period of administration as President
of the South was full of trouble for Sun Yat Sen.
The Yunnanese mercenaries terrorized the whole
population. The President, as usual, was short of money,
despite the taxes levied and the continuation of gambling houses.[1] The mercenaries, not having been paid,
began to raid the stores. Then ensued disorder and pillage. In order to protect themselves, the merchants
formed a Mercantile Defense Corps. Its members wore
uniforms, and with such arms as could be found they
kept guard over the stores. The organization had not
sufficient arms and ammunition for its men, so a depu-
tation was sent to Dr. Sun, and permission was obtained
from him to import a quantity. A shipment came
earlier than could have been the case if the arms had
not been ordered before permission had been given; in
addition to this, there had arrived about three times the
quantity which had been authorized. At once the suspicion of the President and his advisers was aroused,
that the arms were to be used against the government.

---

[1] This is denied by his friends. Sun had closed the gambling houses
in Canton and Nanking when he was in undisturbed power.

The shipment was seized. The merchants were enraged, and in retaliation they closed the approaches to the streets occupied by them and refused to do business. This was the Chinese method of boycott so long in use by the guilds against those who offended them. The merchants were, in fact, in a state of rebellion against the authority of the President.

If the Russian, Borodin, who was at this time the chief adviser of Dr. Sun, did not instigate the policy of the seizure of the arms, he must have been cognizant of it. Sun, it must be remembered, was beset by enemies, worried by disturbances, and undoubtedly suffering from the disease which, two years later, carried him off. He had two thousand loyal Cantonese troops on whom he could rely; they were ordered to clear up the situation. They surrounded the streets which had been closed, and some shooting ensued; then a fire—for which Sun was blamed, whether it originated by his order or not—destroyed a part of the crowded city and caused great loss and suffering.

The trouble with the Yunnanese still remained. To get rid of them he used the stratagem of withdrawing his loyal soldiers across the Pearl River to the island of Honan, which is formed by two branches of the river. It is about twelve miles long and quite narrow, resembling somewhat Manhattan. In addition, he ordered all the thousands of river boats and junks to leave the Canton side and come over to the island. Then the place where the obnoxious Yunnanese were stationed was subjected to a rigorous bombardment. Finding their position untenable and being cut off from supplies, the mercenaries retired to their own province.

The foreigners of Shameen and Hongkong had suffered severely at times from strikes, boycotts, and disturbed conditions; but the inhabitants of Canton, numbering over a million, had suffered far more through pillage, conflagration, and danger to their lives. So on all sides Sun Yat Sen was blamed.

The situation in the province of Kwangtung from Sun's return in February, 1923, until his departure in November, 1924, was deplorable. As President he had control of the northern and western parts of the province, but General Chen held the southern and eastern portions.

Sun despaired of establishing order and peace in the distracted country; and having failed to obtain help from any of the Powers, he turned more and more to the Russians. But his understanding with them did not stop him from seeking any other means which might possibly bring peace and unification to China. He had been in communication with Peking from time to time, and in 1924 he made arrangements for a conference with the government in the north. In November of that year he went to Peking as an envoy from the south; there he could meet not only the Chinese officials, but also the representatives of the Powers.

Not long before Sun left Canton for the north, he had an attack of illness during which he lost consciousness for some time; and he and his advisers were alarmed. Doctors, who afterward examined him in Peking, believed that this was caused by an internal hemorrhage.

A Chinese, a graduate of Harvard, who lived in Peking during 1924–25, has told the writer of conditions in that city at the time. He belonged to a club composed of Cantonese, but even at the meetings of its members the name of Dr. Sun was scarcely mentioned. Outside, they did not speak of him at all; to have done so would have laid them open to suspicion that they were his partisans, and would have placed them in danger, for there were spies everywhere. The club had among its members many men who had been educated abroad; some were American citizens, having been born in the United States. While they were careful what they said even to each other, their opinion was that Sun was a sincere man and a staunch patriot but that he was mistaken in supposing that China was ready for a real democratic government.

On Sun's arrival in Peking, he consulted a physician who placed him in the hospital of the Peking Union Medical College, supported by the Rockefeller Foundation. There he was told that before an opinion could be given, it would be necessary to have an exploratory operation. To this he submitted. The exploration showed that the disease, cancer, had involved the liver and other organs and that it was useless or practically impossible to operate; and the incision was closed.[1] Sun remained in the hospital a few weeks, his sufferings being relieved as much as possible. Peacefully, on March 12, 1925, he died.

His body was first taken to a building in Central Park, where, in a hall, an "altar of sacrifice" for Confucian rites had been erected, before which the coffin was placed. Behind it was a large portrait of the dead leader, and the room was filled with flowers. On the day of the funeral, April 5, the coffin was conveyed to the assembly hall of the Peking Union Medical Col-

[1] This information was given the writer by Dr. M. F. Chung, who was present.

**SUN YAT SEN**

The last picture of him, taken 1925.

lege; there a screen was erected behind it, on which was hung the portrait surrounded by an immense floral wreath. At the request of the widow, a Christian memorial service was held. An address was delivered by George C. Hsu, concerning which a Chinese magazine, publishing a picture of this service, printed the note: "The speaker proved Dr. Sun was a follower, and a revolutionary follower, of Jesus Christ."

In this connection a letter to the writer from the Rt. Rev. Logan R. Roots, of the American Episcopal Church, Bishop of Hankow, contains the following passage:

> Dr. Kung, a descendant of Confucius, told me that he was with Sun Yat Sen when he was dying. Dr. Sun put his hand outside the bedclothes and those standing by thought he did this unconsciously, so they placed his hand under the clothes. He at once put his hand outside again and beckoned to Dr. Kung, who bent over him. Dr. Sun then said in a low voice, "I want it to be known that I die a Christian."

His widow's request for a Christian service was made because she knew it would be his wish.

When the ceremonies were over, the funeral procession marched through the streets, along which immense crowds were gathered. The portrait was carried in front of the hearse, which was followed by troops, carriages, automobiles, and a multitude of friends. The site selected as a temporary resting place for the coffin was the Pi Yun Monastery at West Hills, ten miles west of Peking, and five from the Summer Palace. A niche had been prepared, to which led a long flight of stone steps. Over the center of these steps planks had been laid, and by means of ropes in the hands of Kuomingtang leaders the coffin was pulled up to the niche. There it was deposited, and above it the portrait was placed.

Memorial services were held in various cities in China, and all over the world where there were Chinese. In Honolulu there was an impressive ceremony, a striking feature of which was the gathering of the numerous families who came from the village where Dr. Sun was born. On the first anniversary of his death, March 12, 1926, a memorial service was held in Tai Ho Tien, the former imperial palace, at which Dr. Sun's grandchildren were present. One of them spoke, thanking the people for attending and urging them to continue the unfinished work of their grandfather. On the anniversary date, it has now become an established custom to hold memorial services wherever there are many Chinese residents.

The day before his death, Sun Yat Sen dictated in the presence of witnesses, directions to his followers and to his family, usually called his will. The portion addressed to his followers is read at the anniversary memorial services and at other times. Printed in Chinese and English, it has had extensive circulation. The official translations follow:[1]

[1] NOTE: Attention is called to the words of Sun Yat Sen in the first line of the *Instructions,* where he says that for forty years he has labored unceasingly for the Revolution. As this was dictated in 1925, forty years carries one back to 1885, which is the year in which he mutilated the idols at Choy Hung. It was there said, as shown in chapter v, that the revolution began at that time and by that act. The writer had not seen the *Instructions* when that chapter was written, but Sun's own words indicate the conjecture that he was a rebel from that time onward to be correct.

## THE LAST INSTRUCTIONS OF DR. SUN YAT SEN
### TO HIS FOLLOWERS

For forty years, I have labored unceasingly for the Cause of my countrymen's Revolution, the aim of which is to secure Liberty and Equality in China. The experience accumulated during these forty years profoundly convinces me of the fact that, in order to accomplish this aim, it is absolutely necessary to awaken the multitudinous people, and to unite with those races of the world, which treat us as equals, to strive together.

At present the Revolution is not a complete success. It behooves my fellow-workers to follow the principles and policies which I have set forth in my published works, as: "The Plan for National Reconstruction," "The General Principles of Reconstruction," "The Fundamentals of Democracy," and the "Manifesto of the First National Convention of Representatives," with continued effort, so that the aim may be completely achieved.

That which has been advocated very recently, namely: the calling of a People's Conference and the abrogation of the existing unjust and unfair treaties, must be carried out within the shortest period of time. This is my earnest instruction.

[*Signed*] SUN WEN.

March 11, 1925.

## THE LAST INSTRUCTION OF DR. SUN YAT SEN
### TO HIS FAMILY

Because I have devoted myself to the service of the nation, I did not have time to work for my family. The books, clothes, the house, and other personal belongings that I have are to be left to my wife, Sun Hing Ling, as tokens of remembrance. My son and daughters have grown up. They can stand on their own feet. I sincerely hope that each one of them will take good care of himself or herself, and continue the work that I have undertaken to do. This is my instruction.

[*Signed*] SUN WEN.

These documents were drafted by Wang Ching Wei, at the dictation of Sun Yat Sen in the presence of Mrs. Sun Yat Sen, Sun Fo,[1] Chao Yuen Chung, and others, and signed on March 11, 1925, at Peking. After forty years as a revolutionist, with many opportunities for procuring money, Sun died a poor man. As one writer says: "In China this is considered the best proof of his honesty that can be found."

In China extraordinary reverence is paid to Sun Yat Sen by the Nationalists, who believe they are carrying out his principles. Around his name and memory a cult has grown up. On Monday mornings the attendants at all schools and the employees in all public offices bow three times before his picture, on each side of which hang flags, and sometimes a scroll on which are characters meaning: "The Father of the Republic." The homage paid to him is said by men who know Chinese customs to be greater than that accorded to an ancestor and not unlike that rendered to Confucius. At all public meetings, the same ceremony is enacted and the will is read.

When the Nationalists conquered central China and made Nanking the capital, it was determined to build a magnificent tomb for the final resting place of the great revolutionist. It is situated on a hillside on the outskirts of the city, in a plot of ground surrounded by trees. An imposing flight of steps leads to the circular structure which contains the casket; before it there is an altar for religious rites according to Chinese custom. The architecture of the mausoleum is Chinese, not an imitation of western styles. Multitudes visit the monument—not only those who sympathize with his doctrines

---

[1] Sun Fo, the son by his first wife, was then Mayor of Canton.

and look upon him as the Father of the Republic, but thousands of others.

Some time before the death of Sun Yat Sen, his followers often referred to him as Chung San (Mandarin Chung Shan). These words mean literally the "middle mountain." When in Japan, Sun frequently assumed the name Nakayama, which has the same meaning; and the Chinese adopted its equivalent represented by characters, which may be spelled Chung San in English. A mountain in the province of Shensi, famous in classical writings, bears this name; and Sun may have called himself after it because of a significance attached to it. It may mean the mountain of the Middle Kingdom, as the Chinese Empire was called, because it was supposed to be in the middle of the earth. So the name may signify to the Chinese scholar, "Important as the Mountain of the Middle Kingdom," conveying the idea of towering above others. A Chinese fortune teller in Canton, a story runs, once told Sun that he would become the most important man in China, and that may have suggested the use of the name.

It must not be imagined, however, that all Chinese, or even all Cantonese, thought Sun of such importance or were in agreement with his revolutionary activities. This was the case abroad as well as in China, though people in the south were careful to keep their ideas to themselves. Travelers in various parts of China tell of doubts concerning the Republic, in the minds of many people. Graft and corruption, as they observed them, had certainly not lessened since the change of government; a republic in name had not bettered conditions created by war lords and their lust for power. But whatever opinions some of the Chinese hold, they will not disagree with the ideal of what the Commonwealth of China should be, as Sun set it forth. A scroll of characters written by him has been reproduced in facsimile and widely distributed; it is frequently displayed on the platforms, when Nationalist meetings are held, and read aloud in conjunction with Sun's will. Many have imagined that what he wrote about the Commonwealth was his own composition, but it was really taken from Confucius. Men versed in classical Chinese say that, judging by his formation of characters, Sun was not a good Chinese scholar, but that as he grew older he constantly improved—as is evident from the characters on this scroll. The translation of them into English is not easy and there are some differences of opinion as to the best way to express some of the meanings. The version which commends itself as conforming to English idiom is as follows:

Reason has its sway, the world is a commonwealth. The worthy and the able are alone called to office, and sincerity and harmony are the principal objects sought for. Hence men do not love only their own parents or their own children. There are provisions for the aged, work for the able-bodied, education for the young, and sustenance for the widows, orphans, childless men and women, the defective and diseased. All the males are given proper work and all the females have their homes. The people try hardest to extract wealth from the ground, but not necessarily for their private uses; they exert their utmost effort in labor, but not necessarily for their own benefit. The result is that selfishness, scheming and monopoly are not seen; robbery, theft, violence, and wrongdoing are unknown; and doors and gates remain open day and night. This is called the great Commonwealth.[1]

Some Chinese scholars say that the use of the word commonwealth is a mistake, that Confucius was describ-

[1] Confucius, *Book of Rites.*

ing the ideal social life. But it is evident that in using the passage Sun applied it to his idea of a perfect national life.

Sun Yat Sen aroused a national consciousness in many individuals, but the vast masses were not reached. He had the vision of China as a powerful nation, and nothing was allowed to dim that vision. He did more to awaken China out of its sleep of ages than any other one man; and his power over the hearts and minds of his countrymen has proved greater after his death than it was when he was living.

Sun believed in the capacity of the Chinese for self-government and he was right in his judgment as far as their mental qualifications, their industry, and their business ability are concerned, but he overlooked other necessary qualifications. He made the mistake of judging other Chinese by himself when he considered them ready for a republic. From boyhood he had associated with Chinese who had been in contact with western men and women, and he took them to represent the whole of the people of China. In Honolulu, in Hongkong, and in his travels about the world, his friends were those who had lived under foreign governments and had been educated abroad; and they, in a measure, appreciated his ideas and understood something of democracy. He appeared to think that the mass of people in China were as ready as his intimate friends to understand and value constitutional government.

Further, he did not seem to have formed a correct estimate of the ingrained corruption and chicanery of the official caste. He often treated them as if they were as sincere and honest as himself. He trusted Yuan Shih Kai, General Chen, and others, to his mortification and the undoing of his cherished hopes. While the Chinese are singularly honorable in their business affairs when a bargain is made, yet they have been notoriously corrupt in political affairs.

Henry T. Hodgkin well says that what China needs is:[1] first, strong constitutional government; second, higher moral standards among public men; third, improved communications; fourth, strengthened educational work; fifth, development of her own industrial system; sixth, reorganization of the judicial system.

All these things Sun advocated, and when he was able tried to promote them. He would have agreed with Hodgkin, who wrote further: "The West must give China time to work out her own salvation, must understand China better, must give her fair play, must show her the best of western civilization."

Whatever changes may occur in China, the work begun by Sun Yat Sen will go on. The antiforeign and antichristian feeling will die down as it did in Japan. The day when this occurs will be hastened by manifestations, on the part of foreigners, of good will, justice, and the renunciation of grasping and aggressive policies. There are abundant signs that the Powers now desire to understand China. They have shown a patience and restraint which would have been impossible a few years ago. The fire which Sun Yat Sen started will not be quenched, but will continue until a new China shall emerge to take a rightful place among the family of nations.

[1] *China in the Family of Nations,* p. 234.

# Bibliography

Cantlie, James. Sun Yat Sen and the Awakening of China (London: Jarrold and Sons, 1912).

Coleman, F. E. The Far East Unveiled (London: Cassell and Co., 1918).

Dingle, Edwin. China's Revolution: 1911–1912 (Shanghai: Commercial Press, 1912).

Dixon, C. C. Melbourne to Moscow (London: George Bles, 1925).

Dutcher, George M. Political Awakening in the East (New York: The Abingdon Press, 1925).

Farjenel, Fernand. Through the Chinese Revolution. Translated from the French (New York: F. A. Stokes, 1916).

High, Stanley. China's Place in the Sun (London: The Macmillan Company, 1924).

Hodgkin, Henry T. China in the Family of Nations (New York: Geo. H. Doran, 1923).

Hutchinson, Paul. What and Why in China (New York: Willett, Clark and Colby, 1927).

King-Hall, Stephen. China (London: Methuen, 1924).

Latourette, K. S. The Development of China (New York and Boston: Houghton Mifflin, 1929).

Linebarger, Paul M. Sun Yat Sen and the Chinese Revolution (New York: Century Company, 1925).

McCormick, Frederick. The Flowery Republic (New York: D. Appleton and Co., 1913).

Reinsch, Paul S. An American Diplomat in China (New York: Doubleday, Page Company, 1922).

Soothill, W. E. China and the West (London: Oxford University Press, 1925).

——Timothy Richard, the Most Disinterested Adviser China Ever Had (London: Seeley, Service and Co., 1924).

Sun Yat Sen. The International Development of China (New York: G. P. Putnam's Sons, 1922).

—— Memoirs of a Chinese Revolutionist. A Program for the Reconstruction of China (Philadelphia: McKay, 1929).

—— The Three Principles of the People (Shanghai: Commercial Press, 1928).

Tcheng, Soumay. A Girl in China (New York: Frederick A. Stokes, 1922).

Tyau, M. Y. Z. China Awakened (New York: Macmillan Company, 1922).

Weal, Putnam. The Fight for the Republic in China (New York: Dodd Mead Company, 1917).

—— The Vanished Empire (London: Macmillan Company, 1926).

—— Why China Sees Red (Dodd Mead Company, 1925).

Also sundry copies of the following newspapers:

The *China Press*. Shanghai.

The *Tientsin Times*. Tientsin.

The *Shun Pao*. Shanghai.

The *Honolulu Advertiser*. Honolulu.

San Francisco newspapers.

The *Strand Magazine*. London.

The foregoing is a partial list of books and papers which have been consulted by the author.

# Index

Ah Mi, 3, 6, 11, 12, 17, 21, 46, 75, 125–127
Ai, C. K., 18, 21, 30, 49, 138
Alice Memorial Hospital, 29
Allen, Y. J., 57
Allies, 135
Aloha, 102
American Bible Society, 99
American Pretender, 117
Americans, 123, 146, 152
Anglo-American Hospital, 27
Assembly, of the Republic, 97, 112, 113, 116, 120
Atkinson, A. L. C., 8
Au, Rev. F. C., 54
Australia, 122

Bache, Victor, 49
Belgians, 146
Borodin, Michael, 143–145, 150
Bow Wong Society, 70, 75
Boxer movement, 66, 74
Boycott, Chinese, 34, 146, 150, 151
British, 30, 68, 146; in Hawaii, 14
Buck Dai, 4, 24

California, University of, 111
Cantlie, Dr. James, 29, 30, 47, 50–52, 54, 104, 105; quoted, 32, 48
Canton Christian College, 141
Capitalism, 137
Chang Chau, 3, 82, 83, 85, 86, 92, 94, 129 n.
Chang family, 3
Chang Hwa Republic, 67
Chao Yuen Chung, 156
Chen Chiung Ming, General, 139, 140, 141, 143, 151, 159
Chen, Eugene, 1, 144, 145; quoted, 2
Chicago, 103

Chicherin, 143, 144
*China,* 97
China, division of, 57, 75, 137, 139, 147; and monarchical government, 121; needs of, 160; and republicanism, 101; self-sufficiency of, 66; stagnation of, 33; unity of, 139, 140; and World War, 134–135; *see also* Republic of China
*China Press,* quoted, 2 n.
Chinese, and education, 123; and patriotism, 74; and western civilization, 58, 71–72, 90, 98, 159
Chinese Society of English Education, 77
Choy Hung, 4, 154
Christianity, as basis of reform, 98; and rebellion, 44
Chun, Mr., 99, 100
Chung, Consul General, 77
Chung, Dr. M. F., 152 n.
Chung San, 157
College of Medicine, in Hongkong, 28, 29
Commonwealth of China, 158
Confucianism, 5, 44, 152
Confucius, 22, 156, 158

Damon, Rev. Frank, 49, 101
Democracy, 33, 39, 136
Despotism, 91
*Diocesan Magazine,* 17; quoted, 14

Education, mass, 140
"Educational Society," 35, 39; petitions of, 35–36; and revolution, 36–37
Emma, Dowager Queen, 16
Empire of China, abrogation of, 121

Empress, Dowager, 36, 58, 59, 65, 66, 90, 97; edicts of, 112–113
Extraterritoriality, 45, 56

Farjenel, F., 115; quoted, 114
Father of the Republic, 156, 157
Feng Kuo Chang, 134
Foochow, 105
France, 66, 67, 99, 115, 145
French Revolution, 37
Fukien, 71, 139, 140

George, Lloyd, 134
Germany, 66, 120, 134, 135
Gnone Hap, 67
God Worshipers, Society of, 40
Goodnow, Dr. F. J., 120, 121
Gordon, Captain Charles, 40
Government, constitutional, 75, 140, 159; monarchical, 75, 120, 121
Great Britain, 18, 53, 66, 143, 145, 147; and Hawaii, 14
Guilds, 33, 34, 35, 150

Hagar, Mr., 29
Haiphong, 92, 93
Hankow, 70, 109
Hanoi, 93
Hori, Teiichi, 99, 101, 102; quoted, 99–101
Hsien Feng, Emperor, 65
Hsu, George C., 153
Huang Hsing, General, 112 n., 118, 119; see also Wang Hing
Hung Chung Hui, 48, 82
Hung Siu Tsuen, 39, 40
Hupeh, 91

Idols, mutilation of, 25, 26, 37, 154
Imperial Government, 74, 75, 94, 105, 109
Indo-China, 31
International Development of China, 136, 145
Ioffe, Adoff, 142, 144; quoted, 142

Iolani, 12, 13, 15, 16, 72, 102, 126
Italy, 145

Japan, 57, 66, 99, 103, 119, 120, 123, 135, 145; and extraterritoriality, 45, 56; and modern methods, 45, 57, 90, 101
Japanese, 68, 74, 146
Japanese War, of 1894–95, 65; of 1904–5, 90

Kalakaua, King, 16
Kamehameha IV, 12, 16
Kamehameha V, 12
Kang Yu Wei, 58, 59, 121, 134
Kansas City, 103
Kelly, Kate, 7
Kerr, Dr. John L., 27, 28
Keum Fah, 25
Kobe, 45
Krupps, 116
Kuang Hsu, Emperor, 58, 121; edicts of, 58
Kuhio, Prince, 114
Kung, Dr., 153
Kwangsi, 139, 142
Kwangtung, 1, 2, 151

Lai-lin, 91
Lea, Homer, 59, 103
Lee, Dr., 117
Li Chung, 48
Li Hung Chang, 58
Liliuokalani, 14
Loans, foreign, 116, 145
London, 17, 50–54, 117, 126
London Missionary Society, 5, 18
London Times, 53
Luke Chan, 3, 22, 24 n., 25, 43, 43 n., 111, 122
Luke Ho Tung, 23, 24, 26, 28, 34, 41–43, 111
Lu Szu, 28

Macao, 31, 33, 69, 118, 119, 127, 128
McCartney, Sir Halliday, 51, 52
McCormick, Frederick, quoted, 114

Manchus, 6, 24, 37, 39, 40, 41, 42, 55, 57, 61, 74, 75, 76, 89, 90–91, 103, 106, 107, 119; abdication of, 110, 112–113, 120; armies of, 68; dynasty, 23, 38, 72, 103, 147; government, 31, 35, 36, 53, 62, 106, 110; number of, 62; policy of, 101; and revolutionists, 75
Mandarins, 41, 57; language of, 140
Marryat, Captain, quoted, 9
Marseilles, 106
Meheula, Solomon, 12
Memorials, for Sun Yat Sen, 153–154
Mencius, 39
Mercantile Defense Corps, 149
Militarism, 136
Ming dynasty, 61, 113
Missions, 13, 29, 83, 98; and spirit of revolt, 34
Mohammedans, 135
Mohammedan Uprising of 1857–74, 105
Moji, 119
Moochow, 118

Naaman, 23
Nagasaki, 119, 138
Nakayama, 157
Nakimura, 56
Nanking, 106, 115
"Napoleon for China," 24
Nationalism, 62, 71, 74, 75, 113, 123, 140, 142, 146, 159
Nationalists, 130, 144, 156, 158
New York, 103
North China, 116, 135, 139–141, 145, 146

Okuma, Count, 100

Pakhoi, 92
Paris, 106
Parliament, of China, 97, 141
Patriotism, 72, 74
Peking, 106, 112, 116, 120, 130
Peking Government, 43, 68, 134, 140, 141, 145

Peking Union Medical College, 152
People's Conference, 155
Ping-heon, 91
Pi Yun Monastery, 153
Po Lun, Prince, 76, 77
Portugal, 145
Pott, Mrs. Francis Hawkes, 71
Powers, Treaty, 56, 57, 75, 113, 116, 136, 137, 139, 145, 151, 160; and intervention, 147
Progressive Chinese Society, 48, 82, 92, 100
Progressive Party, 68, 90, 91, 119, 140; in Hawaii, 81; Navy, 92–94
Provincial Councils, 120

Rebellion of 1913, 119
Redfield, William C., quoted, 138
Reform, constitutional, 70, 89; need of, 57, 72, 97; of 1898, 58–59, 65, 90, 121; of 1906, 90, 91
Reform Cadets, 59–60
Reinsch, Paul S., 135, 137
Republic of China, 56, 62, 70, 75, 81, 101, 103, 105, 157; abolition of, 120; its capital, 106, 113, 120; its constitution, 110, 113, 120; finances of, 114; flag, 111; recognition by Powers, 113–114; restored, 121; and U.S., 106; see also China
Republicanism, 13, 14, 50, 89, 91, 119, 121, 145
Revolt, of 1895, 41–42, 68, 111; of 1900, 68–71; of 1904, 81–87, 90; of 1907, 89–95; of 1911, 72, 103–107, 109
Revolution, beginning of, 26, 74, 154
Revolutionists, 70, 78, 92, 127
Richard, Rev. Timothy, 57
Rockefeller Foundation, 152
Roots, Rt. Rev. Logan R., 153
Rousseau, 37
Russia, 66, 120, 142, 144–147

Russians, 142, 143, 151
Russo-Japanese War, 90

St. John's College, 71, 72
St. Louis, 103
Salisbury, Lord, 52
Sandalwood Islands, 11
Sandwich Islands, 11
San Francisco, 76, 103
*San Francisco Examiner,* quoted, 77 n.
Schools, agricultural, 35, 111; American, 98; British, 98; medical, 98
Schurman, Jacob Gould, 147
Scotland Yard, 52
Seattle, 103
Shameen, 86, 150
Shanghai, 71, 105, 106, 120, 121, 129, 136
Shao Chang Lee, Professor, 54 n.
Sianfu, 105
Singapore, 51, 55, 89, 122
South China, 116, 118, 121, 124; Republic of, 144; its Parliament, 139; and Powers, 136
Sovietism, 142–144, 146
Spokane, 103
Straits Settlements, 51, 55, 89
*Strand Magazine,* quoted, 17, 18, 46
"Student Movement," 72
Sun Fo, 111, 156
Sung Hing Ling, 125, 129, 141, 155
Sun Tat Sung, 2, 5–7
Sun Wen, 35–36, 67, 105–106, 122, 155
Sun Yat Sen, American citizen, 6, 76, 117; birth, 7–9, 46, 76; and Christianity, 18, 44, 100, 102, 153; death, 152; Director of Canton Government, 129; Director of Railroads, 115, 122; disguises, 45, 47–48, 57, 85–86, 94, 118; family of, 46, 75, 125–131; finances of, 67, 104, 122; an idealist, 94, 98–99, 101; Liberator of China, 106; Malay blood, 46; marriages, 28, 125, 128–130; names of, 36, 51, 102, 104, 157; President of Chinese Republic, 76, 105, 106, 110, 111, 127; President of South, 129, 139, 143, 149; published works, 155; a republican, 14, 50, 91; a revolutionist, 5, 38, 66; a traitor, 117; in U.S., 49, 50, 59, 76, 77, 103; will, 36, 154–155, 158; quoted, 18, 50, 51, 53, 54, 60–61, 74, 75, 98, 113, 117–119, 135, 136, 142
Swatow, 91
Szechuan, 121

Tai Cheong, 3, 4; baptism, 5, 29; becomes Sun Yat Sen, 31; and Christianity, 16–17, 26, 27; in Hawaii, 6, 12; and idolatry, 16, 22–23, 25; and Manchus, 24; marriage, 28–29; practices medicine, 31, 32; and republicanism, 13; schooling, 5, 11–19; and spirit of rebellion, 16, 26, 30–31
Tai Ho Tien, 154
Taiping Rebellion, 6, 24, 39, 40, 105
Takano, S., 102
Tin Hau, 25
Tokyo, 70
Tong Choy, 70
Tong Phong, 29, 77, 104
Tonkin, 91, 93, 94, 99
*Tuchuns,* 134
Tuck Mung, 29
Twenty-one Demands, of Japan, 135

United States, 45, 46, 67, 99, 103, 147; and Hawaii, 11, 13, 14; and Republic of China, 114
United States Experiment Station in Hawaii, 111

Waichow, 70
Wang Ching Wei, 156
Wang Hing, General, 91, 103, 112, 118

Waseda University, 100
West Hills, 153
Whampoa Military Academy, 146
Wilcox, Dr. E. V., 111
Willis, Bishop Alfred, 12, 13, 16, 126; quoted, 14, 17
Wilson, President, 102
World War, 134, 135, 142
Wuchang, 103, 105
Wu Pei Fu, General, 140
Wu Ting Fang, 44, 117

Yamchow, 103

Yamen, 41, 83, 84
Yap, W., 49
Yap See Yung, 126
Yi Ho, 117
Y.M.C.A. of Canton, 146
Yokohama, 73, 99
Young China, 32–35, 68, 72, 111
Yuan Shih Kai, 58, 109, 111–118, 120, 159; death, 121; as Emperor, 120–121; in Korea, 115; President of Repub'', 110, 113, 120; successors, 134
Yunnan, 94, 121, 142, 149, 150

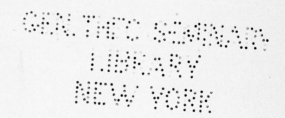